THE PERIODIC TABLE OF

MARVEL

WRITTEN BY
MELANIE SCOTT

CONTENTS

INTRODUCTION

The world of Marvel is a place that is full of fantastical science. While many of the amazing beings that inhabit this Multiverse are far beyond anything we know of from our own lives, when we drill down into the theories behind their powers, they are based on real scientific ideas. The way that radiation can alter humans at a cellular level or genetic modification can change DNA or genius inventors try to construct suits that will enable them to fly … these are all found in the Marvel universe and the real world alike. Science is affecting life on Earth all the time, changing it rapidly both for the better and for the worse.

For many of Marvel's heroes and villains, their abilities are something they are born with—the building blocks are already there in their genes before they enter the world. These characters include the X-Men and the Inhumans, and many others who draw their ancestry from species with certain attributes not found in the humans of Earth. Some are not born but built, with robots and androids symbolizing the cutting edge of human (or alien) invention but also raising the question of where true life begins.

Other characters have powers thrust upon them through scientific experimentation, sometimes when an accident occurs or the process has an unexpected outcome. For example, when Bruce Banner becomes the Hulk after a radiation accident; the Fantastic Four emerge following a space voyage that goes wrong; or Peter Parker is bitten by a certain unusual spider. Both heroes and villains are found in this cohort, as the individual must decide how to move forward with their new abilities and whether to use them for the greater good or their own advancement.

Some use what might be termed "the science of magic," with Earth's greatest minds concluding that sorcery could be just a way of describing processes that are not yet understood by regular science.

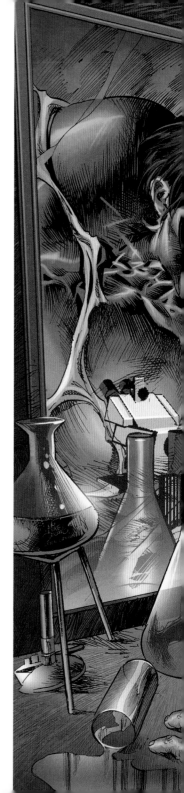

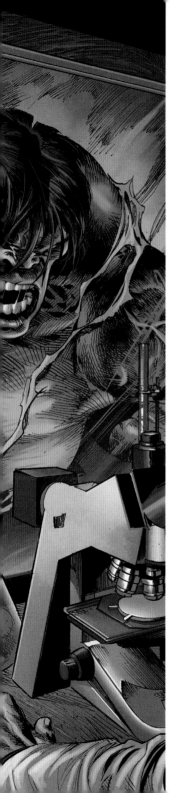

However, many humans become extraordinary through nothing more than utilizing their natural skill to its fullest potential. These are frequently the bravest of all—those who must keep pushing themselves in training so that they are fit to face the most formidable opponents. These peak humans, such as Iron Man and Hawkeye, represent the living embodiment of the theory of "survival of the fittest."

Just like the periodic table of elements, the Marvel Multiverse can be broken down into a number of key commonalities that underpin all the amazing beings who inhabit it. As different characters grow and make their life's journeys, they evolve into individuals of infinite variety, but the vital building blocks of their abilities remain a foundation for their uniqueness.

HOW TO EXPLORE THIS BOOK

The Periodic Table of Marvel is intended to offer fans and newcomers alike the chance to look at the Marvel Multiverse from a whole new perspective. Instead of being grouped by team affiliation or chronological order of appearance, the characters in this book are presented according to the common factors that make them so special—the fundamental basis for their powers or skills. Each chapter comprises a scientific grouping, with more specific commonalities linked within it. Every character has their own periodic table reference, with a unique symbol comprising a code of letters, and an "atomic number" linked to their first appearance as relating to other characters in their chapter. They are also classified as either bonding agents, combustible, stable, toxic, or volatile, depending on the behavioral properties they predominantly exhibit.

Order of appearance in the Marvel Comics Universe when empowered

Properties

1 **Vo**

H

Hulk

Name

Symbol

RADIOACTIVITY

As humans learn to harness the immense power of the atom, both for energy creation and weapons of war, they must also deal with the literal and physical fallout. For many, a brush with high levels of radiation means sickness or even death, but for a select few, it bestows superhuman abilities. These powers can be a blessing or a curse.

Ga GAMMA

The effects of gamma radiation on human physiology have proven to increase strength and durability, pushing them to unprecedented levels.

1 Vo	12 Vo	9 Vo	8 Vo	7 Vo	20 Vo	10 Vo
H	**Sh**	**Ab**	**Rh**	**Le**	**Ma**	**Ds**
Hulk	She-Hulk	Abomination	Rhino	Leader	Maestro	Doc Samson

25 Vo	33 St	26 Vo	30 Vo	21 Vo	29 Vo	41 Vo
Sk	**Ac**	**Rk**	**Rs**	**Rv**	**Ab**	**Ao**
Skaar	Amadeus Cho	Red Hulk	Red She-Hulk	Ravage	Aberration	A-Bomb

38 Vo	45 Vo
Hl	**Tz**
Half-Life	Todd Ziller

SPIDER-INFUSED

Radioactivity channeled through the body of a spider has the effect of giving powers that are specifically associated with arachnids.

2 St	11 St	14 St	32 St	13 St	27 St	31 St
Sm	**Sw**	**Mw**	**Gs**	**Ha**	**Sn**	**Si**
Spider-Man (Peter Parker)	Spider-Woman	Madame Web	Ghost-Spider	Spider-Ham	The Spider-Man	Silk

23 St	24 St	19 Vo	34 St	43 St	44 St	40 Re
Sg	**Sq**	**Dg**	**Sl**	**Uk**	**Md**	**To**
Spider-Girl	Spider-Queen	Doppelgänger	Spiderling	Spider-UK	Mayday Parker	The Other

39 Vo
Tm
The Thousand

WASTE

The by-product of harnessing atomic power is radioactive waste, which, incorrectly treated, can cause superhuman abilities to manifest in some individuals.

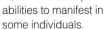

6 St	22 St	4 Vo
Dd	**Jj**	**Sa**
Daredevil	Jessica Jones	Sandman

OVERDOSE

While humans tolerate low levels of radiation every day, excessive levels can trigger dramatic and permanent changes to physiology.

28 St	3 Vo	5 Vo	42 Tx	35 Vo	37 St	36 St
Bm	**Rm**	**Mm**	**Hz**	**Su**	**Fs**	**Dm**
Blue Marvel	Radioactive Man	Molecule Man	Hazmat	Sunfire	Firestar	3-D Man

POWER BROKER PROCESS

The criminal businessman Power Broker uses radioactivity to augment ordinary people and exploit them for profit in entertainment or criminal pursuits.

18 St	17 Vo	15 Vo
Us	**Bt**	**Ar**
U.S.Agent	Battlestar	Armadillo

HULK

REAL NAME: Bruce Banner **POWERS:** Super-strength, stamina, and durability; regenerative healing factor; resurrection **FIRST APPEARANCE:** *Incredible Hulk* #1 (May 1962)

1	Vo
H	
Hulk	

Of all the characters in the Marvel Universe, none embody the property of volatility more than the Hulk. Since the day introverted scientist Bruce Banner takes the full force of a gamma radiation explosion to save an innocent teenager, he spends most of his time locked in internal battle with his rage-fueled alter ego.

As a young man, Bruce Banner agrees to work on a gamma bomb for the US military, conducting testing in the remote desert of New Mexico. When he inadvertently gets caught in a test explosion, Banner's body is subjected to an intense bombardment of highly charged radioactive particles. He should have been killed, but some latent genetic factor in his body instead causes him to develop the capability of turning into a super-strong giant— a "Hulk," as he is dubbed by the shocked soldiers who run into him after his first transformation.

The radioactive blast he is subjected to gives Banner almost unbeatable strength in his green Hulk form. His strength is technically limitless and increases exponentially as he gets angrier. His stamina is also raised to superhuman levels as a result of the effect of the gamma rays on his physiology, and he can leap vast distances. He possesses an extraordinary regenerative healing factor that is even shown to be able to bring him back from the dead. This uncanny ability leads to the discovery that Banner is inherently connected to the source of all the world's gamma radiation, found in the Below-Place. This hellish region exists at the deepest layer of the Multiverse and is linked to the real world via a metaphysical barrier known as the Green Door.

However, all that power comes at the expense of self-control. In his early days, Hulk's rampages cause so much

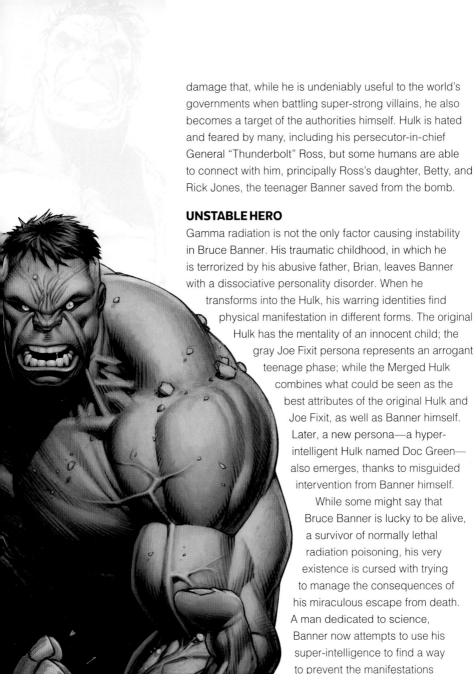

damage that, while he is undeniably useful to the world's governments when battling super-strong villains, he also becomes a target of the authorities himself. Hulk is hated and feared by many, including his persecutor-in-chief General "Thunderbolt" Ross, but some humans are able to connect with him, principally Ross's daughter, Betty, and Rick Jones, the teenager Banner saved from the bomb.

UNSTABLE HERO

Gamma radiation is not the only factor causing instability in Bruce Banner. His traumatic childhood, in which he is terrorized by his abusive father, Brian, leaves Banner with a dissociative personality disorder. When he transforms into the Hulk, his warring identities find physical manifestation in different forms. The original Hulk has the mentality of an innocent child; the gray Joe Fixit persona represents an arrogant teenager phase; while the Merged Hulk combines what could be seen as the best attributes of the original Hulk and Joe Fixit, as well as Banner himself. Later, a new persona—a hyper-intelligent Hulk named Doc Green—also emerges, thanks to misguided intervention from Banner himself. While some might say that Bruce Banner is lucky to be alive, a survivor of normally lethal radiation poisoning, his very existence is cursed with trying to manage the consequences of his miraculous escape from death. A man dedicated to science, Banner now attempts to use his super-intelligence to find a way to prevent the manifestations of his personal trauma from destroying innocent lives.

SHE-HULK

REAL NAME: Jennifer Walters **POWERS:** Super-strength, speed, and durability; regenerative healing factor **FIRST APPEARANCE:** *Savage She-Hulk* #1 (Feb 1980)

12	Vo
Sh	
She-Hulk	

The dose of gamma radiation that creates She-Hulk is markedly less than that which spawns the original Hulk, and instead of being transferred through the air in energy waves, it comes from contaminated blood. It is perhaps these variations in delivery of gamma powers that cause the difference in manifestation between Jennifer Walters and her cousin Bruce Banner.

When Walters is shot by a mobster, Banner steps in to save her with a transfusion of his own blood. This loving gesture saves her life, but the gamma radiation coursing through the donated blood will change Walters forever. Like her cousin, she is transformed into a super-strong green behemoth, naturally known as She-Hulk. Unlike her unfortunate cousin, she retains all her mental faculties and humanity while transformed, while her strength levels are less than his.

GREEN POWER

Where Bruce Banner's existence as Hulk is characterized by mental strife and being hunted by the authorities, Jennifer

Walters has a more stable relationship with her other self. She-Hulk remains in control, except in extreme circumstances when she can become overwhelmed by rage. She is strong, confident, popular, and witty—everything Walters aspires to. Her career in law is still able to continue successfully, and she becomes an asset to several Super Hero teams over the years. After an encounter with a Celestial, She-Hulk's gamma levels are increased and her Hulk form becomes even larger and stronger. However, when in this form, she loses her intelligence and eloquence, becoming more like her cousin Banner's original "Savage Hulk."

After enhancement from a Celestial, She-Hulk can unleash omnidirectional blasts of pure gamma energy, powerful enough to destroy whole city blocks.

ABOMINATION

REAL NAME: Emil Blonsky **POWERS:** Super-strength, stamina, and durability; regenerative healing factor **FIRST APPEARANCE:** *Tales to Astonish* #90 (Apr 1967)

The so-called Abomination is created when communist agent Emil Blonsky sneaks into Bruce Banner's lab. Unwittingly given a huge dose of gamma rays—larger even than that which creates the Hulk—Blonsky is permanently transformed by the radiation into an outsize green monster and soon lives up to his nickname "Abomination." The extreme gamma radiation that triggers his transformation means that he reaches a level of strength even greater than the Hulk. Additionally, Abomination retains his full mental faculties in his monstrous form. However, unlike Banner, he is unable to change back to a human state. Blaming Hulk for his plight, Abomination clashes with his nemesis many times, but his initial strength advantage is canceled out when Hulk gets sufficiently angry.

RHINO

REAL NAME: Aleksei Sytsevich **POWERS:** Super-strength, stamina, and durability, enhanced by polymer suit **FIRST APPEARANCE:** *Amazing Spider-Man* #41 (Oct 1966)

The Rhino is the result of a potent admixture of chemicals and gamma ray bombardment, leaving him with incredible strength and durability. Originally a thug in the pay of the Russian mafia, Aleksei Sytsevich agrees to undergo intense radiation treatments to become hired muscle for a spy ring. In addition to the enormous increase in strength the gamma rays give him, Aleksei is bonded with an ultra-tough, gray, horned polymer suit, leading him to adopt the name Rhino. Rhino frequently clashes with Spider-Man and fellow gamma-enhanced human the Hulk, whose strength he cannot match. Rhino manages to shed his suit more than once and, after many difficult years as a Super Villain, attempts to go straight, but the super-strength bestowed on him by the gamma rays will stay with him forever.

LEADER

REAL NAME: Samuel Sterns **POWERS:** Super-intelligence; telepathy; telekinesis
FIRST APPEARANCE: *Tales to Astonish* #62 (Dec 1964)

Samuel Sterns is living proof that gamma mutations do not always result in super-strength. In Sterns's case, accidental exposure to gamma radiation caused massive growth, not in muscles but in his intellect. Previously an individual of below-average intelligence, Sterns became the Leader, a man with a superhuman brain. His cranium grew to accommodate his increased mental capacity, and his skin turned green, the one instance in which his gamma transformation resembled that of Bruce Banner. The Leader's mastery of any subject known to humankind means that he can design and build any device he needs. His ability to infer the probabilities of any given situation means that he can virtually predict the future. He has also demonstrated telekinesis and mind-control over weak individuals.

MAESTRO

REAL NAME: Bruce Banner **POWERS:** Super-strength; resurrection **UNIVERSE:** Earth-9200
FIRST APPEARANCE: *Hulk: Future Imperfect* #1 (Dec 1992)

Maestro is an alternate-future Bruce Banner, and, as such, was exposed to the same gamma explosion as his Earth-616 counterpart. However, in Maestro's reality, Earth is devastated by a nuclear war, the radioactive fallout from which makes him even stronger than the Hulk. His mental state is also far less stable than the original, perhaps due to the increased radiation exposure, or the trauma of living in his war-ravaged reality. Maestro, who lives a century ahead of the original Bruce Banner, fights and schemes his way to become the tyrannical ruler of a society called Dystopia. Maestro has battled Hulk, getting the upper hand not only due to his superior strength and battle experience but also because he doesn't care how much damage he causes or how many innocent civilians he hurts.

DOC SAMSON

REAL NAME: Leonard Samson **POWERS:** Super-strength, stamina, and durability; resistance to injury **FIRST APPEARANCE:** *Incredible Hulk* #141 (Jul 1971)

Psychiatrist Dr. Leonard Samson uses gamma energy siphoned from Bruce Banner to give himself similar powers. The dose of radiation is less than that which creates the Hulk, so Doc Samson's strength is also proportionately less, although still at a superhuman level. Doc Samson's strength level is unaffected by his emotions, but it appears to be affected by the length of his hair, like the Biblical character his name references. Like Hulk and other gamma mutates, Samson can be resurrected via his link to the Green Door. On one occasion, he is unable to resurrect his own body but manages to come back using the body of Alpha Flight member Sasquatch. Doc Samson devotes much of his life to helping "cure" Bruce Banner. He occasionally uses his gamma powers to be a Super Hero himself.

SKAAR

REAL NAME: Skaar **POWERS:** Super-strength, stamina, and durability; connection to the Old Power **FIRST APPEARANCE:** *World War Hulk* #5 (Nov 2007)

As the son of Hulk, Skaar inherits his father's gamma-fueled powers. These attributes strongly resemble those of his father: incredible strength, stamina, and durability, plus green skin. On his maternal side, Skaar is descended from the Shadow People of the planet Sakaar and, as such, also possesses the Old Power, a synthesized but highly unstable version of the Power Cosmic. The Old Power is an energy that allows Skaar to connect with his world and manipulate its elements, including lava, and take on a stone form. Skaar has an extremely high tolerance to heat since he was born from a cocoon inside a radioactive lake of fire. Later, on Earth, Skaar is stripped of his gamma powers when his father, as Doc Green, injects him with a serum made from Banner's blood, although he retains his Old Power.

AMADEUS CHO

33   St
Am
Amadeus Cho

REAL NAME: Amadeus Cho **POWERS:** Super-strength, durability, stamina; healing factor; genius intellect **FIRST APPEARANCE:** *Totally Awesome Hulk* #1 (Feb 2016)

Amadeus Cho uses his precocious intelligence to devise a way of protecting the original Hulk by using nanites to siphon off excess radiation. Then, he alters the cells in his own body with nanobots, enabling him to contain and use gamma energy from the Hulk without destroying himself in the process. He develops powers similar to Bruce Banner's, but, like Banner, Cho struggles to contain Hulk's destructive impulses and so leaves Earth until he can figure out the problem. The solution comes again in the form of counteracting nanobots administered by his friends, which protect his cells from the gamma but prevent him from using it. Cho emerges as a more slimline, more stable version of Hulk.

RED HULK

26   Vo
Rk
Red Hulk

REAL NAME: General Thaddeus Ross **POWERS:** Super-strength, durability, and speed; healing factor; emits gamma radiation **FIRST APPEARANCE:** *Hulk* #1 (Mar 2008)

Having devoted his life to hunting down the Hulk, General Thaddeus "Thunderbolt" Ross undergoes his own gamma transformation to become the Red Hulk.

The secretive process uses Bruce Banner's body and energy drained from the Hulk to allow Ross to mutate into a super-strong being just like his nemesis—but with red skin. Unlike Hulk, Ross can move between his human and Red Hulk forms at will and retains his mental faculties as Red Hulk. Also as he gets angrier, Ross's body becomes hotter and emits more radiation and can reach levels at which he becomes dangerously unstable and vulnerable.

RED SHE-HULK

30   Vo
Rs
Red She-Hulk

REAL NAME: Betty Ross **POWERS:** Super-strength, stamina, and durability; energy absorption and emission **FIRST APPEARANCE:** *Hulk* #15 (Sep 2009)

Betty Ross becomes a miracle of science in more than one way: After being killed by the Abomination, Bruce Banner's former wife is resurrected by M.O.D.O.K. and then subjected to gamma radiation that changes her into the highly volatile Red She-Hulk. Betty transforms into Red She-Hulk when sufficiently angry; however, the unpredictable effects of gamma on her physiology put her at risk of being permanently transformed. In addition to superhuman strength, durability, and stamina, Red She-Hulk can absorb energy and transmit it with a touch and possesses highly corrosive saliva. Red She-Hulk is depowered by the Doc Green incarnation of Hulk as he tries to eradicate all gamma mutates on Earth.

RAVAGE

21	Vo
Rv	
Ravage	

REAL NAME: Geoffrey Crawford **POWERS:** Super-strength and durability; healing factor **FIRST APPEARANCE:** *Rampaging Hulk* #2 (Sep 1998)

Wheelchair-bound physics professor Geoffrey Crawford finds a way to replicate former pupil Bruce Banner's genetics to restore his body to health. Using a telepod machine to dissipate his body into pure energy then reassemble it, he rewrites his DNA to mimic Banner's. Crawford emerges as Ravage, a version of the Hulk that retains his mental capacity. This enables him to defeat Hulk in their first clash. Ravage's powers fade in daylight, but he reengineers pods that make his transformation permanent. However, unlike Hulk, Ravage's strength does not increase with his anger; he is defeated by the Green Goliath when they next meet and is captured by the US military.

ABERRATION

29	Vo
Ar	
Aberration	

REAL NAME: Rana Philips **POWERS:** Super-strength; gamma emission **FIRST APPEARANCE:** *Incredible Hulk* #601 (Aug 2009)

Sentenced to death after mistreating prisoners of war, former military police officer Rana Philips agrees to take part in an experiment to enhance her physiology with genetic material from the superhuman Abomination. The untried procedure is carried out by the Origins Corporation, set up by Norman Osborn to monetize the synthesizing of superhuman abilities. However, the corporation has not been able to perfect the infusion of the gamma DNA, and it acts like a cancer on Philips's body, causing her to grow larger and more mutated. Once her systems start breaking down, there is nothing that can be done, and Aberration does not survive a battle with Hulk's daughter from the future, Lyra.

ANCILLARY EXEMPLARS

41	Vo
Ao	
A-Bomb	

38	Vo
Hl	
Half-Life	

45	Vo
Tz	
Todd Ziller	

One of the most notable ancillary exemplars of the effects of gamma radiation is **A-Bomb**, also known as Rick Jones. Saved by Bruce Banner from the gamma explosion that creates the original Hulk, Jones is later kidnapped by the Leader and M.O.D.O.K. and infused with DNA from the blood of the Abomination, which turns him into the hulking blue hero A-Bomb. He is later depowered by Doc Green. Other gamma mutates include **Half-Life**, a college professor who is turned into a vampire-like being that drains the life-force of others, and **Todd Ziller**, a US army corporal who is given a recombinant serum mixing gamma radiation with the Super-Soldier Serum and Pym Particles, which turns him into an aggressive, giant reptile.

SPIDER-MAN

2	St
Sm	
Spider-Man (Peter Parker)	

REAL NAME: Peter Parker **POWERS:** Super-strength, durability, stamina, and agility; healing factor; wall-crawling; spider-sense
FIRST APPEARANCE: *Amazing Fantasy* #15 (Jun 1962)

When radioactivity is channeled through the body of an arachnid, it can have very different effects on the human body than regular radiation. The best known example of a person enhanced by this kind of spider-infused radiation is Peter Parker, the original Spider-Man. Parker is still a schoolboy, attending a demonstration of an atomic ray, when he is bitten by a spider that has passed through the ray and absorbed a lethal dose. As the creature dies, it bites the young man on the hand. Parker immediately notices a burning sensation and the glowing appearance of the spider, and, shortly afterward, begins to feel strange sensations in his body. He can now scale the sides of buildings and crush metal with his bare hands. Testing out his new abilities in the wrestling ring, Parker discovers that he has the proportionate strength of a spider as well as its speed and agility. He uses his natural aptitude for science and invention to build devices that fire out a substance similar to a spider's web, which he uses to swing between the buildings of New York City.

GREAT POWER

Spider-Man also has a sixth sense that alerts him when danger is near. This, coupled with superhuman reflexes, means that it is very difficult for his opponents to land a punch on him. His spider-sense is instinctive, but he has more control over his other arachnid abilities. These include wall-crawling—Spider-Man can make any part of his body stick to a surface regardless of its alignment. The dead spider's irradiated venom enables Peter Parker to mentally control subatomic particles in his body and cling to surfaces.

Spider-Man's other notable abilities include superhuman stamina and durability, which allow him

to endure far tougher situations than regular people. His body does not produce fatigue toxins as quickly as others, so he doesn't tire easily. He can also take much more physical punishment than the average human. These qualities are demonstrated on one occasion when Spider-Man is able to recover his strength and effectively "rest" while simultaneously being beaten up by several of Doctor Octopus's henchmen. The radiation in his blood also makes him resistant to many blood-borne diseases and toxins.

While Spider-Man's powers come from the venom of an irradiated spider, they are also linked at a deeper level to the Web of Life and Destiny, a fifth-dimensional structure linking all the realities of the Multiverse. Here, the godlike Spider-Totems select suitable avatars for their powers in various universes—Peter Parker is one of the chosen ones on Earth-616. Thus, all spider-infused individuals in the Multiverse owe their abilities not only to science but also to something more mystical.

After his life is changed forever by the radioactive spider's bite, Peter Parker uses his great power to become one of Earth's leading heroes. His formidable abilities, coupled with his good heart, make him the ultimate example of a spider-powered individual among the many that exist in the Multiverse.

SPIDER-WOMAN

REAL NAME: Jessica Drew **POWERS:** Super-strength, stamina, durability, and agility; wall-crawling; bioelectric blasts; pheromone secretion **FIRST APPEARANCE:** *Marvel Spotlight* #32 (Feb 1967)

11   St

Sw

Spider-Woman

Like Spider-Man, Jessica Drew is a spider-infused individual, although her abilities do not come from a radioactive spider bite. As a child, Drew contracts uranium poisoning after undergoing her scientist father's experiments with the High Evolutionary in Transia. To save her, Drew's father injects her with a serum made from the blood of rare spiders— species that are known to possess regenerative qualities. She is then sealed in a genetic accelerator for many years, her aging process slowed while her body adapts to the radiation and assimilates the spiders' blood. When she wakes years later, Jessica is no longer fully human, genetically speaking. She is a Spider-Woman.

SPIDER SPY

While her dual nature makes it difficult for her to be accepted in many places, the arachnid powers Jessica has acquired make her an excellent candidate for certain secretive organizations. She is now superhumanly strong and agile,

has elevated levels of stamina and durability, and can crawl up vertical surfaces. Spider-Woman can also fire bioelectric "Venom Blasts." She sometimes secretes pheromones that trigger strong sensations in others, like fear, and she has total resistance to radiation, a healing factor, and super-hearing—another sought-after espionage skill. When Spider-Woman later has a child, Gerry, he inherits her unique DNA and with it her powers, including wall-crawling, Venom Blasts, and pheromone secretion.

Unlike many spider-infused individuals, Spider-Woman has the ability to fire powerful bioelectric blasts through her hands.

MADAME WEB

REAL NAME: Julia Carpenter **POWERS:** Superhuman sense of touch; wall-crawling; psionic web creation; precognition **FIRST APPEARANCE:** *Marvel Super Heroes Secret Wars* #6 (Jun 1984)

Julia Carpenter is given spider powers as part of a secret initiative called the Commission on Superhuman Activities, which is set up to create Super Heroes who are more compliant with the authorities. Tricked into subjecting herself to a series of spider-venom injections, Julia finds that she has powers similar to Peter Parker's—she can cling to walls, she is super-strong and fast, and she has the agility and reflexes common to spider-infused individuals. However, in some key aspects, Carpenter's powers have different scientific roots to Spider-Man's. Many of them are psionic—mind-controlled—including a unique form of webbing that she can will into existence and direct with the power of thought. She also has a superhuman sense of touch and can feel the slightest vibrations around her.

BLIND SEER

After the death of the blind psychic Madame Web, Carpenter inherits Web's ability to see the future—as well as her sightlessness. She also becomes capable of astral projection and develops the ability to read minds. Carpenter can now use her powers to act as an early-warning system when danger threatens heroes connected to the Web of Life and Destiny. Unlike her predecessor, Carpenter retains the use of her legs as Madame Web, meaning she is less vulnerable to attack. She can also fight while blind, using her knowledge of hand-to-hand combat and her precognitive abilities to hold her own against even the toughest opponents.

When Julia Carpenter finds the original Madame Web close to death, Web transfers her psychic powers and her blindness to Carpenter.

GHOST-SPIDER

REAL NAME: Gwen Stacy **POWERS:** Super-strength, durability, and stamina; healing factor; wall-crawling; spider-sense **FIRST APPEARANCE:** *Edge of Spider-Verse* #2 (Sep 2014)

32   St

Gs

Ghost-Spider

On Earth-65, it is high-school student Gwen Stacy, not Peter Parker, who is bitten by a spider at a demonstration of radioactivity. She develops super-strength, agility, speed, and the ability to crawl up walls. Like other spider-infused heroes, she also has a sixth "spidey-sense" alerting her to danger. At first taking the name Spider-Woman, she is given web-shooting tech by retired hero The Wasp.

Upon being given the Interdimensional Travel Watch, Gwen can move between different realities within the Multiverse. She later uses this device to conduct different lives in different universes. She continues her Super Hero life on Earth-65, while trying to experience a more normal life on Earth-616, attending college under a secret identity.

POWER PLAYS

Gwen Stacy later discovers that the spider that gave her her powers was genetically engineered by Earth-65's Cindy Moon. This version of Cindy later injects Stacy with a formula designed to remove her

spider powers. Gwen is able to restore them using radioactive isotopes extracted from the DNA of extraterrestrial spiders, but the effects are limited. She eventually finds a new way of restoring her powers—by bonding with a symbiote created using genetic material from the alien spiders and the Lizard Formula.

After taking the name Ghost-Spider, Stacy becomes a founding member of the Web-Warriors, a group of spider-infused heroes protecting the Web of Life and Destiny that links the Multiverse.

Ghost-Spider adopts a secret identity as a regular Empire State University student in Earth-616 but remains a spider-infused Super Hero in Earth-65.

SPIDER-HAM

REAL NAME: Peter Porker **POWERS:** Super-strength; wall-crawling; invulnerability to injury **FIRST APPEARANCE:** *Marvel Tails Starring Peter Porker the Spectacular Spider-Ham* #1 (Nov 1983)

Peter Porker, the Spectacular Spider-Ham, starts life as an ordinary spider living in the basement of eccentric scientist May Porker on Earth-8311. When she tests her new atomic hairdryer on herself, May becomes radioactive and bites the spider, transforming him from a spider into a pig. Although the radiation has the effect of changing his shape, Porker retains the abilities he had as a spider, including wall-crawling and impressive strength. He takes on May Porker's surname and acquires her flair for science, which enables him to build gadgets that shoot web-lines he can swing on. In Spider-Ham's universe, the laws of physics are more "cartoonish." For example, if he is crushed, he will be flattened and then bounce back. He can also summon weapons out of thin air.

SPIDER-MAN NOIR

REAL NAME: Peter Parker **POWERS:** Super-strength, speed, agility, and balance; healing factor; organic web-line creation **FIRST APPEARANCE:** *Spider-Man Noir* #1 (Dec 2008)

On Earth-90214, Peter Parker lives in Depression-era New York City, working as an assistant to a newspaper photographer. One night, Parker comes across a group of gangsters at the docks unloading stolen statues that are said to bestow a curse on anyone who touches them. Inside the statues are hundreds of spiders that escape and attack one of the crooks, killing him with their venom. When one spider finds and bites the concealed Peter, it does not kill him. Instead, he is "cursed" with spider powers, which he promptly begins using to address the societal problems caused by the poverty that he sees around him. The Spider-Man, as he calls himself, can shoot web-lines from his own wrists. Unlike most other spider-infused heroes, he is also willing to use firearms on occasion.

SILK

REAL NAME: Cindy Moon **POWERS:** Super-strength; wall-crawling; organic web-line creation; Silk-sense **FIRST APPEARANCE:** *Amazing Spider-Man Vol. 3* #1 (Apr 2014)

Cindy Moon is bitten by the same irradiated spider that bites Peter Parker and turns him into Spider-Man. Like Parker, she immediately develops spider powers following the bite. Although her spider-infused skills are generally very similar to Parker's, Cindy's super-strength manifests at a slightly lower level. However, her "Silk-sense"—her version of Spider-Man's spider-sense, which warns of danger—is more elevated than that of any other Spider-Totem. She can also produce her own webbing from her forearms. The fact that she shares the origin of her powers with Spider-Man means that Silk can always sense where Peter Parker is across all realities of the Multiverse.

SPIDER-GIRL

REAL NAME: Anya Corazon **POWERS:** Super-strength, speed, and stamina; wall-crawling; web creation **FIRST APPEARANCE:** *Amazing Fantasy Vol. 2* #1 (Aug 2004)

When Anya Corazon is given powers by a sorcerer from the mysterious Spider Society, she gains super-strength, stamina, speed, and reflexes, plus wall-crawling abilities and even a tough exoskeleton, although she later loses this in battle. Her powers at this time stem from the Spirit of the Hunter—a mystical force that Corazon, or Araña, as she first calls herself, carries within her. But when she chooses to pass the Spirit of the Hunter on, she loses her spider-infused powers. Sometime later, Anya is infected with a Spider-Virus by the Jackal, and the effects of radioactive spider venom reproduce in her system, granting "Spider-Girl" a copy of Peter Parker's spider powers as well as organic web creation.

SPIDER-QUEEN

REAL NAME: Adriana Soria **POWERS:** Telepathy; telekinesis; shape-shifting **FIRST APPEARANCE:** *Spectacular Spider-Man Vol. 2* #15 (Aug 2004)

After being chosen for a top-secret program to create advanced soldiers during World War II, Adriana Soria mutates into a new species of human: *Homo insectus*. The procedure uses radiation to activate a strand of DNA dating back to when the human branch of the evolutionary tree split off from that of the insects. This gives Soria power over all insects, as well as any humans who still possess latent insect genes. Her saliva contains a substance that gives spider powers to ordinary people and transforms them into monstrous spider-beings. She also has psionic powers and is connected to the multidimensional Web of Life and Destiny.

DOPPELGÄNGER

19	Vo
Dg	
Doppelgänger	

REAL NAME: Unknown **POWERS:** Super-strength, durability, and stamina; razor-sharp web-line creation **FIRST APPEARANCE:** *Infinity War* #1 (Jun 1992)

Doppelgänger is a "shade" of Spider-Man, an evil copy created by the evil Magus using extradimensional M-Bodies. Although Magus creates shades of many Super Heroes, Doppelgänger is the only one known to have survived the Infinity War. The creature is not an exact replica of the original Spider-Man and differs in a few key ways. He has six arms, giving him the same number of limbs as a spider; talons; and jagged, fanglike teeth. Doppelgänger also fires razor-sharp webbing and is stronger than Spider-Man but significantly less intelligent.

SPIDERLING

34	St
Sl	
Spiderling	

REAL NAME: Anna-May Parker **POWERS:** Wall-crawling; advanced spider-sense **FIRST APPEARANCE:** *Amazing Spider-Man: Renew Your Vows Vol. 2* #4 (Feb 2017)

Anna-May Parker is the daughter of Peter Parker and Mary Jane Watson on Earth-18119. The radioactive spider venom that got into her father's system as a young man and alters his DNA also affects Anna-May, who inherits all of his spider-powers, plus an enhanced precognitive spider-sense. As she grows, "Annie" discovers that she has strong links to the Web of Life and Destiny, which holds together the threads of the Multiverse. She is the Patternmaker—the Spider-Totem who has the ability to heal the Web when it breaks.

ANCILLARY EXEMPLARS

43	St
Uk	
Spider-UK	

44	St
Md	
Mayday Parker	

40	Re
To	
The Other	

39	Vo
Tm	
The Thousand	

There are countless other spider-infused beings inhabiting the Multiverse. One of the key individuals is **Spider-UK**, a British hero who is a leading recruiter for the Spider-Army. He has similar powers to the original Spider-Man but no spider-sense. Elsewhere in the Multiverse is

Mayday Parker, Earth-982's Spider-Woman and the daughter of the deceased Peter Parker and Mary Jane Watson. **The Other** is a spider deity linked to the Web of Life and Destiny that can bestow its great powers into any receptacle, transforming them into humanlike spider monsters. Meanwhile, **The Thousand**, otherwise known as Carl King, eats the dead irradiated spider that bit Peter Parker, and, instead of gaining Spider-Man's spider powers, his body turns into a voracious hive of spiders.

DAREDEVIL

REAL NAME: Matt Murdock **POWERS:** Superhuman hearing, touch, smell, and taste; heightened reflexes; radar sense
FIRST APPEARANCE: *Daredevil Vol. 1* #1 (Feb 1964)

6	St
Dd	
Daredevil	

As the number of ways in which humans can use the power within atoms grows, so too does the problem of what to do with the highly toxic waste product that results. Such dangerous substances need to be handled extremely carefully and, sadly, accidents happen, with severe effects. However, these effects are not always wholly negative.

When young Matt Murdock leaps to save a blind man from being hit by an out-of-control truck carrying radioactive materials, he gets the man clear of danger but is hit in the face by some of the truck's leaking contents. While in normal individuals, exposure to excessive radiation would cause the degradation of their body's cells, in Matt Murdock, the opposite occurs, with the exception of his eyes. When he wakes in the hospital following the accident, the isotopes in the truck's waste have caused him to lose his sight, but they have heightened his other senses to superhuman levels.

SUPER SENSES

Murdock's hearing is now so acute that he can pick up on someone's heartbeat and use it to identify them. He can also hear the breathing of someone in a different room to him. A handy side effect of these abilities is that he finds it very easy to judge when someone is lying to him, as their heart rate and respiration change. Murdock also finds that he can identify a person by their smell as his olfactory system was equally heightened to superhuman levels by the freak accident.

Murdock's tactile senses are now so sensitive that he is able to read by tracing the ink on the page with his fingertips. He can also detect movement in the air

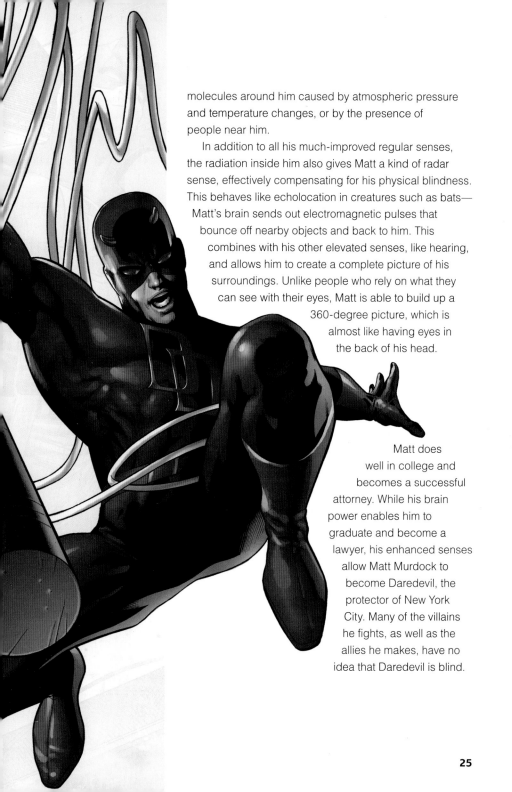

molecules around him caused by atmospheric pressure and temperature changes, or by the presence of people near him.

In addition to all his much-improved regular senses, the radiation inside him also gives Matt a kind of radar sense, effectively compensating for his physical blindness. This behaves like echolocation in creatures such as bats— Matt's brain sends out electromagnetic pulses that bounce off nearby objects and back to him. This combines with his other elevated senses, like hearing, and allows him to create a complete picture of his surroundings. Unlike people who rely on what they can see with their eyes, Matt is able to build up a 360-degree picture, which is almost like having eyes in the back of his head.

Matt does well in college and becomes a successful attorney. While his brain power enables him to graduate and become a lawyer, his enhanced senses allow Matt Murdock to become Daredevil, the protector of New York City. Many of the villains he fights, as well as the allies he makes, have no idea that Daredevil is blind.

JESSICA JONES

REAL NAME: Jessica Jones **POWERS:** Super-strength, durability; flight; healing factor
FIRST APPEARANCE: *Alias* #1 (Nov 2001)

22   St

Jj

Jessica Jones

It appears that Jessica Jones is destined to have her life changed by radioactive waste, and fate will not let her wriggle free. As a high-school student, Jones is saved from being hit by a truck carrying radioactive materials, which bears a strong resemblance to the vehicle that hits Daredevil and gives him superhuman senses. However, soon afterward, in a strange twist of fate, Jones and her family are on a trip when her father loses control of the car and crashes into a convoy of army trucks carrying hazardous material. A can of radioactive waste falls into Jones's lap and the car flips over, bursting into flame. Jessica is the only survivor, but she spends months in a coma. She is woken only when she reacts to a massive power surge caused by the cosmic devourer Galactus as he attempts to consume Earth.

SUPER SLEUTH

Struggling to adjust to her terrible loss, Jessica returns to school at Midtown High. One day, as she is running home

to her new adoptive parents, she discovers that the radioactive waste, possibly triggered by the blast of energy from Galactus, has given her super-powers. Jessica can fly, albeit not very smoothly, and is also super-strong. As an admirer of local heroes the Fantastic Four and Spider-Man, Jessica decides to become a costumed Super Hero. But despite the amazing powers that the radiation has given her, she is not a natural at this job and gives it up to pursue a more low-key career as a private detective.

Instead of using her super-powers as a Super Hero, Jessica Jones decides to become a private detective and sets up her own agency, Alias Investigations.

SANDMAN

REAL NAME: William Baker **POWERS:** Amorphous sand body; super-strength; immortality
FIRST APPEARANCE: *Amazing Spider-Man* #4 (Sep 1963)

4	Vo
Sa	
Sandman	

SANDS OF TIME

Although Sandman's physical abilities makes him a formidable opponent, they also come with inherent weaknesses. Water affects his ability to control his sand particles, as does electricity. Another vulnerability of Sandman's transformation is that his consciousness seems to inhabit just one of the grains of sand in his body. If that particle is kept apart from the others, he cannot reform. Radiation has also given Sandman effective immortality, but when he encounters his multibillion-year-old self from an alternate future, he gets a glimpse of the terrible reality of living such a life.

William Baker, also known as Flint Marko, is a career criminal. Escaping jail, he takes refuge in a cave filled with radioactive medical waste. When the police try and smoke him out, there is a chemical reaction and his body fuses with the irradiated sand underneath him. Back in prison, Baker realizes that his body is changing—it can transform into sand and take on any shape he wants.

Sandman, as he begins calling himself, is delighted at first, as it means that he cannot be contained by any regular police cell. Purely by willing it, he can alter the cohesion of the molecules in his body, splitting them apart or pulling them together to assume an ultra-durable stone-like form. Even when scattered across a wide area, Sandman can retain mental control over the particles of his body and command them to reassemble and reform. He can break himself up into identical clones or become giant-size and reshape parts of his body into weapons like axes and hammers.

Sandman's ability to enlarge his amorphous sand body at will means he can quickly overwhelm regular-size Super Heroes like Spider-Man in battle.

BLUE MARVEL

REAL NAME: Adam Brashear **POWERS:** Super-strength; flight; antimatter manipulation
FIRST APPEARANCE: *Adam: Legend of the Blue Marvel* #1 (Nov 2008)

Adam Brashear is a genius physicist who designs an Antimatter Reactor, which can harness powerful energy from the antimatter universe known as the Negative Zone. However, the device explodes and he is doused in radiation. The exposure gives Brashear incredible powers, including flight, super-strength, and invulnerability, plus the ability to fire blasts of the antimatter energy that now fills his body. Energy from the Negative Zone is several times more powerful than that from the normal universe, and no other human has been able to coexist with it before. The antimatter radiation additionally grants Brashear, who becomes the Super Hero Blue Marvel, near invulnerability, even in outer space, which he can navigate without breathing equipment.

RADIOACTIVE MAN

REAL NAME: Chen Lu **POWERS:** Radiation absorption and emission as heat, light, force fields, or contaminants **FIRST APPEARANCE:** *Journey into Mystery* #93 (Jun 1963)

Chinese scientist Chen Lu is working on a way to use nuclear radiation to induce super-powers in humans. Having formulated a vaccine to protect against the damage that radiation can do to the body, Chen Lu uses himself as a test subject to demonstrate his work to his government sponsors. He exposes himself to massive radioactivity and gains the power to both absorb radiation and project it, with no harm to himself. He can also neutralize attackers who have radiation-based powers and can convert his radioactivity into heat energy or force fields. Because he constantly emits some level of radiation, unless Chen Lu, who comes to be known as Radioactive Man, wears an inhibitor, he causes the deaths of many people from radiation poisoning—both deliberately and by accident.

MOLECULE MAN

REAL NAME: Owen Reece **POWERS:** Molecular manipulation on a seemingly unlimited scale
FIRST APPEARANCE: *Fantastic Four* #20 (Nov 1963)

Owen Reece becomes the Molecule Man when working at ACME Atomics Corporation. He is fixing one of the machines when he is hit by a huge overdose of radiation, caused by the actions of the otherdimensional Beyonders. Following this incident, Owen has the power to rearrange the molecules of anything—a power so great that he fears it and subconsciously imposes limits on himself. Part of this manifests in using a metal "wand" to channel his abilities; the tool is unnecessary but makes Reece feel more in control and at the same time separate from his power. He struggles with his sanity over the years and is eventually captured by Doctor Doom to be used as a source of power after the Multiverse is destroyed. Imprisoned on the surviving fragments, known as Battleworld, Molecule Man is finally discovered by Peter Parker and Miles Morales, who, with the help of Mister Fantastic and his allies, use Molecule Man's power to overthrow the tyrant Doom and rebuild the Multiverse.

ANCILLARY EXEMPLARS

Being radioactive can have terrible consequences for relationships. **Hazmat** discovers her powers when she inadvertently gives her boyfriend radiation poisoning. And not all radioactive beings get their powers from accidents. **Sunfire's** ability to absorb the sun's radiation and use it to fly and fire plasma blasts is his natural power, possibly inherited as a result of his family's exposure to an atomic bomb. **Firestar**, too, is a mutant—she can convert naturally occurring electromagnetic energy to microwave radiation. One of the more unusual radiation-induced transformations is **3-D Man**, who is obliterated in a radioactive explosion but lives on after being preserved as an after-image on his brother's glasses.

U.S.AGENT

REAL NAME: John Walker **POWERS:** Super-strength, stamina, durability, reflexes, and agility
FIRST APPEARANCE: *Captain America* #354 (Jun 1989)

Former soldier John Walker is one of many people to be offered the chance to augment his strength to superhuman levels—at a price. The Power Broker Process is devised by Curtiss Jackson and scientist Dr. Karl Malus to be a variation and upgrade on the Super-Soldier Program. The subject is put into a machine and given doses of certain chemicals mixed with radiation. At the end of the process, they are either superhumanly strong or are turned into deformed beasts and cast into the sewers. There is a 50/50 chance of either outcome, depending on the genetic makeup of the person undergoing the procedure. In Walker's case, he gets lucky and is given strength greater than Captain America's. However, even if the process is successful, participants must take expensive and addictive pills to counteract the procedure's side effects.

A NEW CAREER

Originally, Walker plans to use his new strength to go into wrestling, but he is persuaded that greater opportunity awaits in the world of Super Heroics. After a stint as Super-Patriot, Walker even rises to the heights of carrying the mantle of Captain America, at a time when the authorities want someone more biddable in the role. However, Walker's inherently unstable nature, possibly exacerbated by the Power Broker Process, means that he is eventually sidelined. One fake assassination later, Walker is back— mindwiped, upgraded, and ready for action as U.S.Agent. However, it remains to be seen whether Walker truly has the temperament to be a Super Hero.

Through the Power Broker Process, U.S.Agent gains extreme strength and durability, but it may also have enhanced the unstable side of his nature.

BATTLESTAR

REAL NAME: Lemar Hoskins **POWERS:** Super-strength, stamina, durability, reflexes, and agility
FIRST APPEARANCE: *Captain America* #341 (May 1988)

17   Vo
Bt
Battlestar

Lemar Hoskins serves in the US Army, where he befriends fellow soldier John Walker. After leaving the military, both Walker and Hoskins undergo the Power Broker Process, a procedure for strength augmentation using a combination of radiation and chemicals. Like Walker, Lemar survives the process and becomes superhumanly strong. At first, he uses his new abilities to wrestle but when his friend Walker becomes the Super-Patriot and then Captain America, Lemar joins him, first as a new Bucky and then as Battlestar. Later, Battlestar is kidnapped by the Power Broker and Dr. Karl Malus for a de-augmentation experiment. Emaciated and weak, Battlestar fights back and, with Walker's help, forces Malus to perform the augmentation again, regaining his strength.

ARMADILLO

REAL NAME: Antonio Rodriguez **POWERS:** Super-strength, stamina, and durability; claws
FIRST APPEARANCE: *Captain America* #308 (Aug 1985)

15   Vo
Ar
Armadillo

Ex-con Antonio Rodriguez is desperate to find a cure for his wife's paralysis. Dr. Karl Malus agrees to help him if, in return, Rodriguez undergoes a version of the Power Broker Process and works for him. For Rodriguez's strength enhancement, Malus adds gene splicing using armadillo DNA. Rodriguez becomes super-strong and durable, like other survivors of the Power Broker Process, but in addition he develops a super-tough armored hide like an armadillo, as well as long claws. Armadillo becomes a big hit in the newly formed Unlimited Class Wrestling Federation, which includes only superhumanly strong fighters, but his career runs into trouble when he goes on a rampage in New York City. Armadillo tries for years to find a cure for his condition but eventually must accept the way he is.

EVOLUTIONARY ANOMALIES

While some Super Heroes have superhuman abilities thrust upon them, others are simply born with them. Those possessing the X-gene are mutants, whose wide range of powers generally manifest at puberty. Other individuals acquire powers after their genetic makeup is altered by scientific intervention or have latent genes awoken by other means.

Mu MUTANT

Mutant powers are almost as individual as a fingerprint. Many use their natural abilities to protect humanity, while others see them as a route to power or wealth.

18 Co **W** Wolverine	4 Ba **Px** Professor X	5 St **X** X-Men	6 Vo **M** Magneto	28 Vo **Ap** Apocalypse	24 Vo **Em** White Queen	21 Ba **St** Storm
20 St **Ni** Nightcrawler	19 St **Co** Colossus	25 St **Kt** Shadowcat	26 Re **Rg** Rogue	41 Vo **Ps** Psylocke	45 St **Dz** Dazzler	40 St **Mk** Magik
46 St **Gm** Gambit	44 Vo **My** Mystique	15 Vo **Fr** Powerhouse	29 St **Nx** Mister Sinister	35 Vo **Ak** Summoner	34 Co **Ca** Children of Apocalypse	

MUTATE

Mutates are hybrid individuals who inherit a unique set of powers in their DNA, as well as those who—willingly or not—have their genetics altered by science.

2 Vo **N** Namor the Sub-Mariner	**3** St **Na** Namora	**16** Re **Nm** Namorita	**1** Vo **At** Atlanteans	**8** Co **Aa** Attuma	**22** St **E** Eternals	**23** Vo **Dv** Deviants
36 Vo **Mo** Mole Man	**37** Vo **Ty** Tyrannus	**12** Vo **He** High Evolutionary	**14** Vo **Wk** Warlock	**13** Vo **Mb** Man-Beast	**11** Re **Ne** New Men	**42** Vo **Ay** Ayesha
51 St **Hg** Higher Evolutionary	**47** Co **Nb** Nobilus	**7** Vo **Q** Quicksilver	**30** St **Sg** Squirrel Girl	**17** St **Mn** Mantis	**27** Ba **Cd** Cloak and Dagger	**9** Vo **Sc** Scorpion
39 Vo **Nt** Nitro	**38** Co **M** M.O.D.O.K.					

TERRIGENESIS

Terrigenesis is an ancient process that uses rare crystals found on the moon to activate the latent abilities of the Inhumans and those who share their genes.

10 Ba **In** Inhumans	**31** St **Kk** Ms. Marvel	**32** St **Mg** Moon Girl	**33** St **Uc** Ulysses Cain	**48** Vo **Qk** Quake	**49** St **Kv** Anastasia Kravonoff	**50** Co **Ke** Kei Kawade

EVOLUTIONARY ANOMALIES: MUTANT

WOLVERINE

18	Co
W	
Wolverine	

REAL NAME: James Howlett **POWERS:** Super-strength; claws; Adamantium-enhanced skeleton; healing factor; enhanced senses
FIRST APPEARANCE: *Incredible Hulk* #180 (Oct 1974)

While Wolverine is arguably the alpha specimen of the incredible race of mutant beings known as *Homo superior*, he is exceptional in more ways than one. Although he is born a mutant, Wolverine's natural gifts are also scientifically augmented by the Weapon X program, meaning Wolverine's many deadly attributes can be classified into two categories: innate and man-made.

Wolverine's birth name is James Howlett, although he later takes the alias Logan. He is a mutant with two key abilities: being able to extend long bone claws from his wrists and having an incredibly advanced healing factor that allows him to recover from virtually any injury. This curative capability does a lot more for Wolverine than just clearing up battle injuries. It also improves his stamina, as it eliminates fatigue toxins and accelerates the training of his muscles. Wolverine's extraordinary regenerative powers also enhance his endurance as seen in his super-strength and speed. It slows down the natural process of aging, too, preventing Logan's body from going into decline and allowing him to live for more than a century. Over the years, Wolverine suffers many tragic losses and traumatic events, but his healing factor also works on a psychological level, and he is able to suppress and move on from painful memories with a kind of mental scar tissue.

Like the fierce creatures with which he shares a name, Wolverine's senses are heightened to levels well above those of a normal human. He can see well both in daylight and at night, has excellent hearing, and, most notably, a phenomenal sense of smell that enables him to be

an expert tracker. He can even use his sensitive nose to root out shape-shifters and deduce secret identities.

WEAPON X

When Wolverine is captured by the US government for its Weapon X program, with a view to making him its ultimate weapon, he becomes a living science experiment. Wolverine's mind is wiped and his natural mutant abilities are augmented with the super-strong metal, Adamantium, which is bonded with his skeleton. To any average person, Adamantium would be poisonous, but Wolverine's healing factor means that his body is able to continually fight off the metal's toxins. Now many times heavier than he was before, it is a huge feat of strength for Wolverine just to move his body around.

The Weapon X procedure also brings Wolverine's more feral side to the surface, and the scientists are soon made aware that he will not be an easy weapon to control. He escapes his captivity by flying into a berserker rage—a savage state in which his strength is increased but his humanity is lessened—and killing all the Weapon X personnel who have experimented on him against his will. Wolverine is one of the most fascinating of his kind because he is not just a mutant but also the result of a scientific augmentation process. These two factors combine to make him a formidable example of *Homo superior*, with very few weaknesses.

PROFESSOR X

REAL NAME: Charles Xavier **POWERS:** Telepathy; mind control; mental information transfer
FIRST APPEARANCE: *X-Men* #1 (Sep 1963)

In the history of mutantkind, Charles Xavier is one of the most important individuals on the planet. While his body is confined to a wheelchair, his mind is a supremely powerful tool—and sometimes weapon—capable of reaching out to and influencing almost anyone on Earth. It is perhaps not surprising that Xavier goes against the norms of mutant development, which dictate that mutant powers manifest in childhood. He first exercises his psionic capabilities before he is even born—while in utero, Xavier kills his twin, whom he senses to be evil.

MIND CONTROL

Once his powers have fully developed, Xavier can telepathically connect to anyone within a radius of around 250 miles. He can communicate with and control those with whom his mind is linked, as well as implant information within the thoughts of individuals. Xavier can also use his mental abilities to conceal or disguise himself and make others experience potent hallucinations.

Xavier later begins devising Cerebro, a machine that can harness his telepathy to detect mutants anywhere in the world. His aim is to found a school for young mutants, to turn them into productive members of society. This school, in many cases, will be the only place in the world where mutants feel they fit in. He also prepares training facilities at the school so that a special team can be assembled to combat evil mutants. As Professor X, he becomes the founder, mentor, and teacher of the original X-Men and generations of mutants to follow.

Professor X's hoverchair levitates off the ground, enabling him to negotiate any surface. Its armrests are linked to Cerebro and other advanced devices.

THE X-MEN

FIRST APPEARANCE: *X-Men* #1 (Sep 1963)

The original X-Men are the initial beneficiaries of Professor Charles Xavier's "School for Gifted Youngsters." The very first student at this special institution is Scott Summers, a young mutant who has caused an accident with his powerful eye beams. Xavier's aim for his school is to both protect humanity from harm caused by mutant powers and to protect mutants themselves from the effects of the fear and hatred that their incredible abilities often engender.

GIFTED YOUNGSTERS

While each mutant at Professor X's school has one key shared factor—the so-called X-gene that gives them their abilities—the way in which those abilities manifest is different in every individual. Summers, code-named Cyclops because of his optic blasts, is one of the original X-Men roster that includes the strong but super-intelligent Beast, the ice-wielding Iceman, the winged Angel, and Jean Grey. Grey's power is similar to Xavier's, in that she is an extraordinarily powerful

telepath, but they have key differences in their psionic abilities. While her telepathy is at a lower level than the professor's, unlike him, Grey is also a telekinetic, meaning she is able to move objects with her mind.

The teenagers at Xavier's school learn to control their powers for their own sake, but they also have a wider mission— to promote peaceful relations between regular humans and *Homo superior*, and to eliminate any threats from evil mutants. Despite their good intentions and repeated feats of heroism, the X-Men still find it hard to win the trust and admiration of the humans they are sworn to protect. This outcast status makes it all the more important that they stick together and support each other as a team.

The X-Men roster contains mutants trained and educated by Professor X. Their mission is to protect the world from mutants with less noble intentions.

MAGNETO

REAL NAME: Max Eisenhardt **POWERS:** Magnetism control (of metal objects and electromagnetism in the atmosphere and body) **FIRST APPEARANCE:** X-Men #1 (Sep 1963)

Magneto is an exceptionally powerful mutant who has the ability to control magnetism. This does not just extend to tangible metal objects like the structural parts of buildings, vehicles, and various weapons, although this alone would make him a formidable opponent. Magneto can also control electromagnetism in the atmosphere around him, creating force fields to protect himself or causing disaster-level events in nature.

MASTER OF MAGNETISM

Magneto can also use his control of magnetic fields to fly. By creating opposing magnetic forces that naturally repulse each other, he can push himself away from the ground. Likewise, this aspect of his power can be used to levitate objects. Additionally, he can harness electromagnetism to fire powerful pulses, either as targeted blasts against opponents or to a wider effect, such as knocking out communications devices. Magneto's powers even extend to manipulating the metal and magnetic

elements within the body, affecting the blood or brain-wave functions.

Although he is one of the mightiest mutants on Earth, his powers manifest much later than most of his kind. This may be because, as a Jewish teenager, Max Eisenhardt suffers greatly under the Nazi regime in Europe. Later, as Magneto, Eisenhardt comes to view the persecution of mutants as analogous to anti-Semitism. Setting mutantkind apart from humans, Magneto comes to view *Homo superior* as just that—superior to *Homo sapiens*.

Magneto's ability to manipulate and control any form of magnetism enables him to sustain flight over long distances and shoot deadly rays and pulses.

APOCALYPSE

REAL NAME: En Sabah Nur **POWERS:** Super-strength and durability; immortality; molecular manipulation; psionic powers; energy blasts **FIRST APPEARANCE:** *X-Factor* #5 (May 1986)

One of the oldest mutants known to exist, Apocalypse is born in Ancient Egypt. Although he is cast out by his people due to his gray skin, Apocalypse personifies the evolutionary concept "survival of the fittest" and outlives them all. This immortality is perhaps his most notable mutant power, but it is by no means his only one. He can also rearrange the molecules of his own body, changing its shape and size and healing himself of any wounds. He can absorb energy and redirect it in powerful blasts, and he possesses the ability to move objects, including himself, through the air.

Apocalypse is later able to augment his powerful abilities further by utilizing Celestial technology, after having been infected with a techno-organic virus aboard one of the aliens' ships.

EMMA FROST

REAL NAME: Emma Frost **POWERS:** Telepathy; transformation into organic diamond form; energy blasts **FIRST APPEARANCE:** *X-Men* #129 (Jan 1980)

Emma Frost is an interesting example of a holder of the X-gene due to her manifestation of a secondary mutation. While her primary mutant power is her powerful telepathy, Frost later develops a "diamond form," in which her body transforms into an organic diamond composition, making her much more resistant to physical attacks. As well as increasing her levels of invulnerability, the transformed tissues of her body also give Frost enhanced strength and stamina.

As a telepath, she is almost unrivaled on Earth and is of a similar caliber to Charles Xavier. Frost can manipulate the minds of others to an enormous degree and also shield her own mind against psionic interference. Furthermore, she can use her mind to channel psionic energy, sending it out in powerful blasts.

STORM

REAL NAME: Ororo Munroe **POWERS:** Manipulation and harnessing of Earth's energies **FIRST APPEARANCE:** *Giant-Size X-Men* #1 (May 1975)

As a small child, Ororo Munroe is an African princess fallen on hard times. Her mutant gene activates as she is trekking from Egypt to Kenya, trying to reach her ancestral homeland. Storm, as she becomes known, discovers that she has the power to psionically control the weather, including temperature, moisture levels, and atmospheric pressure around her. This extends to creating or dispersing rain, snow, all forms of wind, and electrical storms. Storm can also harness the energy of these phenomena to fire electrical blasts or freeze objects. Her intense psychic connection to the Earth's energies also gives Storm a special sensitivity to all living organisms and their life-forces.

NIGHTCRAWLER

REAL NAME: Kurt Wagner **POWERS:** Teleportation; adhesive hands and feet; prehensile tail; agility **FIRST APPEARANCE:** *Giant-Size X-Men* #1 (May 1975)

Some mutants outwardly appear to be baseline humans, but Kurt Wagner is not one of them. Born with blue fur, gleaming eyes, pointed ears, and a prehensile tail, Wagner is shunned by ordinary people for his demonlike appearance. However, he is adopted by a circus, where he can display his incredible natural agility. Later, when Wagner is forced to leave this temporary home, his most notable mutant ability manifests—he can teleport. Since this teleportation occurs via another dimension, each time Wagner uses the power, he leaves behind a telltale smell of sulfur. He also has to be very aware of where he is teleporting to, as reappearing inside an object or other hazard could injure him.

COLOSSUS

REAL NAME: Piotr Rasputin **POWERS:** Conversion of his body into a steel-like substance **FIRST APPEARANCE:** *Giant-Size X-Men* #1 (May 1975)

The unusual mutant ability of Piotr Rasputin, aka Colossus, is turning his entire body into a toughened steel-like substance. Although Colossus appears metallic following his transformation, he remains organic. His almost instantaneous metamorphosis is achieved by Colossus willing it and linking himself to a material called osmium, located in another dimension. The carbon atoms within his regular body are then switched out with the osmium atoms, and his transformation is complete. Colossus's strength, durability, and stamina are all enhanced when he is in his "steel" form, and, more surprisingly, so is his speed.

KITTY PRYDE

REAL NAME: Katherine "Kitty" Pryde **POWERS:** Phasing, or intangibility; walking on air or water; invisibility **FIRST APPEARANCE:** *X-Men* #129 (Jan 1980)

Kitty Pryde, aka Shadowcat, is a mutant with the power of intangibility. This means that she can pass the individual atoms that constitute her body through the atoms of something else, enabling her to move with ease through solid objects. She can also use this intangibility or "phasing" to render herself impervious to attacks, allowing solid materials like bullets to pass through her body without injury. Helpfully, if Pryde is in contact with another object or person when she phases, she can phase them with her. She can also use her ability to effectively walk on air or water.

ROGUE

REAL NAME: Anna Marie **POWERS:** Absorption of the energy, memories, and powers of others **FIRST APPEARANCE:** *Avengers Annual* #10 (Aug 1981)

The mutant Rogue has a particularly traumatic manifestation of her power when, as a teenager, she inadvertently puts her boyfriend in a coma. Rogue can absorb and then manifest the life energies and memories of anyone she touches. If that individual has powers, she can take them as well. The effects are not permanent, but they can last a long time if physical contact is prolonged. Initially, Rogue has no control over her absorption ability, leading her to refrain from accidental contact with anyone. Eventually, however, she gains a measure of control over her power.

ANCILLARY EXEMPLARS

A lot of mutants number themselves among the X-Men over the years, and their powers are many and varied. **Psylocke** manifests formidable psionic powers. **Dazzler**, meanwhile, deploys her ability to take in sound and emit light to pursue a second career as a singer, putting on light shows at her concerts. **Magik** is connected to limbo, using it for teleportation, and she is also a sorcerer. Being able to convert potential energy to kinetic energy allows **Gambit** to turn any inanimate object into an explosive device. **Mystique** is a powerful shape-shifter who does not join the X-Men but follows her own, sometimes dangerous, agenda.

FRANKLIN RICHARDS

REAL NAME: Franklin Richards **POWERS:** Reality-warping; telepathy; telekinesis; precognition; astral projection; pocket-universe creation **FIRST APPEARANCE:** *Fantastic Four Annual* #6 (Nov 1968)

to have lived, Richards has vast psionic and cosmic powers, and even the ability to warp reality. It is not surprising that the child of two heroes should be special, but Richards exceeds all expectations. However, when his powers start to fade, the world's greatest minds investigate—and discover that Franklin, aka Powerhouse, never truly possessed the X-gene. In fact, acting on a subconscious desire to be special, he uses his powers to alter his cells so that he appears to be a mutant. Instead of being born *Homo superior*, he is a self-made mutant.

Franklin Richards, the son of two non-mutant Super Heroes—Mister Fantastic and the Invisible Woman—is one of the most intriguing examples of mutant powers in the Marvel Universe. Long believed to be one of the most powerful mutants ever

MISTER SINISTER

REAL NAME: Nathaniel Essex **POWERS:** Super-strength, stamina, and speed; psionic powers; molecular control; healing factor **FIRST APPEARANCE:** *Uncanny X-Men* #221 (Sep 1987)

development of humankind. His research draws the interest of the ancient mutant Apocalypse, who in turn transforms Essex into a mutant himself. Essex uses his expertise to augment his DNA over the years, adding to his capabilities. Like Apocalypse, he can control the molecules in his body to assume different forms and powers as well as heal himself from wounds and disease, making him immortal. Essex also has extensive psionic powers, as well as superhuman physical powers that he took from a dead mutant's DNA.

Nathaniel Essex, or Mister Sinister as he is later known, is a rare example of a mutant chimera—a genetically engineered mutant. As a Victorian-era geneticist, Essex predicts the emergence of mutants as part of the evolutionary

SUMMONER

REAL NAME: None **POWERS:** Invulnerability except for a weakness in his eyes; daemon conjuring; constructing weapons from his body **FIRST APPEARANCE:** *X-Men* #2 (Nov 2019)

35   Vo
Ak
Summoner

The Summoner is a mutant who lives for hundreds of years on the mutant island of Arakko, which long ago was joined to another mutant island, Krakoa. The Summoner's body is invulnerable, with the exception of his eyes. He also has the magical ability to call forth hordes of daemons and construct weapons from a black "ichor" (fluid) that comes from within his own body. The Summoner is able to educate even Apocalypse on mutant lore, informing him that there was a whole generation of mutants before Apocalypse and that he, the Summoner, is Apocalypse's grandson. However, the Summoner cannot be trusted to tell the truth, and his long game is to take Krakoa from the mutants in the name of Arakko, even if he has to betray and attack his own kin to do so.

CHILDREN OF APOCALYPSE

NAMES: War, Pestilence, Famine, and Death **POWERS:** Various and individual (see below)
FIRST APPEARANCE: *Marvel Comics* #1000 (Aug 2019)

34   Co
Ca
Children of
Apocalypse

The ageless mutant tyrant Apocalypse keeps an elite band of warriors known as the Four Horsemen to serve him, but the original iteration of this group are his own children. The Children of Apocalypse are War, Pestilence, Famine, and Death. All mutants, the siblings manifest a range of abilities, including the shared power of longevity. War has power over fire— she is able to combust the air itself and channel the flames through her weapons. Her sister, Pestilence, uses poisoned arrows to infect her victims with a lethal disease, which they in turn can spread to others. Their brother, Death, can end someone's life with a mere glance, while Famine can bring devastation to crops. After his four children are trapped in the demonic dimension of Arenth, Apocalypse builds a pyramid to honor them.

NAMOR

2	Vo
N	
Namor the Sub-Mariner	

REAL NAME: Namor **POWERS:** Amphibious nature; flight; communication with aquatic life-forms **FIRST APPEARANCE:** *Marvel Comics* #1 (Oct 1939)

King Namor would be the first to admit that he is a paramount figure in the world of mutants, and indeed the world in general. He is the remarkable product of a union between a princess of the undersea kingdom of Atlantis and a human. Namor is a combination of the best qualities of his two parents with some added features that are apparently all his own. It is these additional features—wings on his ankles that enable flight and a strength level greater even than other Atlanteans—that have led observers to believe Namor to be not only an Atlantean-human hybrid but also a mutant carrying the X-gene.

It seems that Namor, also known as the Sub-Mariner, is almost impossible to categorize, carrying traits of *Homo sapiens*, *Homo superior*, and *Homo mermanus*. The latter species, that of the Atlanteans, gives Namor his ability to live underwater for unlimited periods and to survive and thrive in the cold, dark ocean. Namor's top swimming speeds vastly eclipse those of other Atlanteans, and he uses a kind of electrolocation to navigate his way through the darkest depths. He has gills for underwater breathing as well as a respiratory system for survival on land, while his general physique is robust enough to withstand the incredibly high pressure on the ocean floor. Namor is capable of communicating telepathically with other Atlanteans and all manner of aquatic life-forms.

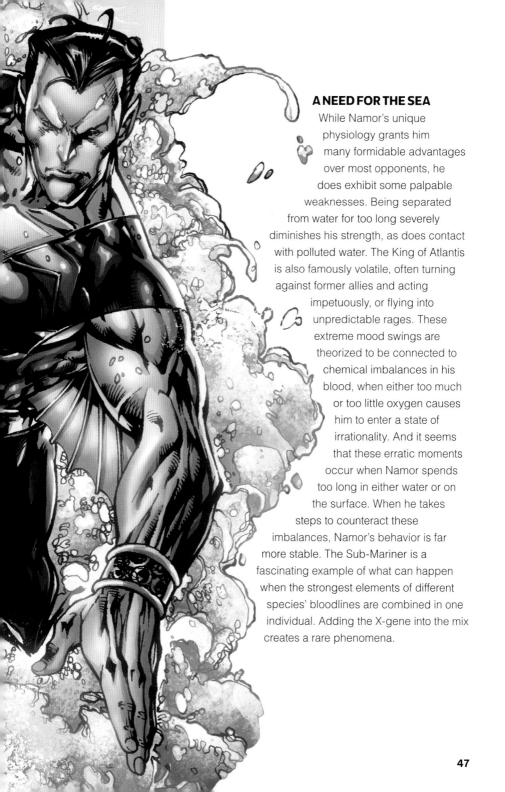

A NEED FOR THE SEA

While Namor's unique physiology grants him many formidable advantages over most opponents, he does exhibit some palpable weaknesses. Being separated from water for too long severely diminishes his strength, as does contact with polluted water. The King of Atlantis is also famously volatile, often turning against former allies and acting impetuously, or flying into unpredictable rages. These extreme mood swings are theorized to be connected to chemical imbalances in his blood, when either too much or too little oxygen causes him to enter a state of irrationality. And it seems that these erratic moments occur when Namor spends too long in either water or on the surface. When he takes steps to counteract these imbalances, Namor's behavior is far more stable. The Sub-Mariner is a fascinating example of what can happen when the strongest elements of different species' bloodlines are combined in one individual. Adding the X-gene into the mix creates a rare phenomena.

NAMORA

REAL NAME: Aquaria Nautica Neptunia **POWERS:** Amphibious nature; super-strength, speed, and stamina; flight; longevity **FIRST APPEARANCE:** *Marvel Mystery Comics* #82 (May 1947)

Like her adoptive cousin Namor, Namora is a unique hybrid of Atlantean genes and human mutant genes. Her mother is a surface-dweller and her father an Atlantean. At first, Namora has the blue skin of her father's kind, but at puberty it changes to the pale skin of her maternal line. She takes the name Namora when she teams up with her cousin to avenge her father, who is killed by divers stealing pearls from Atlantis. Namora can swim faster than most Atlanteans and survive indefinitely on the surface world, though she does become weaker if separated from water for too long. Namora can also live deep in the ocean, suffering no ill effects from the pressures or lack of light. Unlike pureblood Atlanteans, her hybrid vigor gives her a greater healing factor and longevity, while vestigal ankle wings enable her to fly.

NAMORITA

REAL NAME: Namorita "Nita" Prentiss **POWERS:** Amphibious nature; mental communication with aquatic life-forms; super-strength; flight **FIRST APPEARANCE:** *Sub-Mariner* #50 (Jun 1972)

As the clone daughter of Namora, Nita Prentiss shares the hybrid Atlantean-human-mutant physiology of her "mother," and all the strengths and weaknesses that accompany it. However, during the cloning process, extra genes are added to Namorita from Atlantean warriors of the past. This means that her skin does not change color at puberty like Namora's does. This genetic tinkering is also intended to help her avoid the oxygen instability problems suffered by Namor, but it does lead to other issues: Nita's skin turns blue later in life, and her hands and feet become webbed. Later, she evolves again, and her skin blisters and cracks before being shed, revealing her more human form underneath. She shares a mental bond with Namor that allows her to sense him wherever he is.

ATLANTEANS

POWERS: Ability to live underwater, using gills to breathe; super-strength, durability, and speed
FIRST APPEARANCE: *Marvel Comics* #1 (Oct 1939)

The origins of the water-breathing natives of Atlantis—scientific name *Homo mermanus*—are unknown, but one theory suggests that they may be a genetic mutation of *Homo sapiens.* They have many striking biological and physiological differences from the land-dwelling humanoid species. The most obvious is their blue skin. Many other differences are due to the Atlanteans' need to live entirely under the sea. They are extremely rapid swimmers and can navigate the murky depths and intense pressures of the ocean with ease. They are a warlike people when roused to anger, as they frequently are by the manner in which *Homo sapiens* treat the world's oceans. However, their capacity for entering into battle with the surface world is limited by their inability to breathe out of water.

ATTUMA

REAL NAME: Attuma **POWERS:** Amphibious nature; super-strength, speed, stamina, durability, agility, and reflexes; flight **FIRST APPEARANCE:** *Fantastic Four* #33 (Dec 1964)

Attuma is a pureblood Atlantean, although he is one of the exiled barbarian tribe known as the Skarka. He is exceptional among his race, being much stronger than the average *Homo mermanus.* This exceptionality is increased further in an unusual way when, after being killed by the Super Hero Sentry, Attuma is resurrected by Doctor Doom, with some considerable upgrades. Using his unique blend of science and magic, Doom gives Attuma the same capabilities of flight, strength, and air-breathing as Namor, as well as offering him access to advanced technology and weaponry. Although he has spent most of his life at war with Namor for the right to sit on the throne of Atlantis, Attuma eventually allies with his old enemy in order to protect the undersea realm from outside threats.

ETERNALS

POWERS: Super-strength; telepathy; telekinesis; teleportation; flight; cosmic-energy blasts; molecular manipulation; immortality **FIRST APPEARANCE:** *Eternals* #1 (July 1976)

Millennia ago, the godlike alien Celestials are drawn to Earth by the presence of life on the planet. Using their advanced technology, the Celestials bestow cosmic energy on some of the apelike creatures they find, triggering the accelerated development of three distinct races. One of these is the Eternals—*Homo immortalis*—the most elevated of all the Celestial creations.

The Eternals are few in number but extremely powerful and long-lived. Thanks to the cosmic energy in their bodies, they have a number of powers, including flight, psionic abilities, super-strength, and molecular manipulation. An Eternal's power is channeled through their eyes. Though their name suggests otherwise, Eternals can be killed. However, their advanced technology enables them to resurrect themselves. They are also vulnerable to a form of mental illness called the Wy'ry, which, once it takes hold, can be cured only by the destruction of that Eternal.

THE COLLECTIVE

As well as their individual powers, the Eternals also have the capability of coming together to form the Uni-Mind, a collective entity that uses the combined intelligence and energy of all the beings who create it. It is via the Uni-Mind that the Eternals on Earth choose their leader, known as the Prime Eternal.

At first, they keep themselves separate from the other beings on Earth, living on high, remote mountain peaks, but the activities of another Celestial-created race, the Deviants, draws them into war. Later, after many thousands of years, the Eternals also make themselves known to their human relatives, occasionally allying with Super Heroes like the Avengers.

Eternals look human, but the cosmic energy in their bodies allows them to fly, makes them immune to disease, and enables them to live for millennia.

DEVIANTS

POWERS: Greater intelligence, strength, and longevity than average humans; varied and highly individualistic abilities **FIRST APPEARANCE:** *Eternals* #1 (July 1976)

23	Vo
Dv	
Deviants	

Like humans and the Eternals, the Deviants are created as a result of the extraterrestrial beings known as the Celestials imbuing humanoid apes on Earth with cosmic energy. *Homo descendus*, to give the Deviants their scientific name, have unstable DNA as a result of the Celestial experiments, and so they cannot breed individuals with any kind of consistent appearance or set of abilities. Their uniqueness is, ironically, the Deviants' most unifying factor. Although their appearance is unprepossessing, Deviants are not unintelligent—quite the opposite, as they quickly develop the technological know-how to build an empire and dominate ancient humans, who are still little more than cave-dwellers by this point. Deviants fight with the Eternals to defend their hard-earned gains, and even with the Celestials when they return to check the progress of their creations. But the Celestials eventually destroy the Deviant Empire with a cataclysmic flood, driving the Deviants deep underground and fostering their anger and resentment still further.

ANCILLARY EXEMPLARS

36	Vo
Mo	
Mole Man	

37	Vo
Ty	
Tyrannus	

The **Mole Man**, Harvey Elder, is a prime example of rapid evolutionary mutation in action. Living in the underground realm of Subterranea, Mole Man develops a form of radar sense to help him navigate the dark tunnels. He is also able to utilize abandoned Deviant technology and become ruler of the poor unfortunate mutates they leave behind, as well as another underground race known as the Moloids. Another who has made good use of what the Deviants abandon is the villainous **Tyrannus**. Formerly the Roman Emperor Romulus Augustus, Tyrannus uses Deviant technology and former Deviant slaves to launch attacks on the surface world after being banished to Subterranea by the sorcerer Merlin. Tyrannus achieves immortality by drinking from the underground Fountain of Youth and has a range of psionic powers, including telepathy and life-force absorption.

HIGH EVOLUTIONARY

REAL NAME: Herbert Wyndham **POWERS:** Superhuman intelligence; forced evolution or devolution; super-strength; advanced healing factor **FIRST APPEARANCE:** *Thor* #134 (Nov 1966)

A scientist specializing in genetics, the High Evolutionary becomes his own test subject when he uses his Evolutionary Accelerator on himself. The rapid evolution that the machine triggers gives the High Evolutionary superhuman powers, including super-strength and invulnerability when wearing his specially devised armor. Already an intelligent man, his invention enables him to advance his brain to the limits of its full potential. The High Evolutionary can also accelerate or decelerate the development of other organisms. He uses this ability to create his own army of evolved beasts, the New Men. Such is the High Evolutionary's scientific prowess and ambition, he is able to build himself a whole new world—Counter-Earth—occupying an exactly opposite position to Earth in its orbit.

ADAM WARLOCK

REAL NAME: Adam Warlock **POWERS:** Super-strength and speed; flight; telepathy; energy manipulation; cosmic-energy blasts **FIRST APPEARANCE:** *Fantastic Four* #66 (Sep 1967)

In a top-secret research facility, Adam Warlock is created by scientists to be the pinnacle of evolution. Warlock escapes his creators and the High Evolutionary takes him under his wing, guiding him and giving him purpose. He also gives Warlock an Infinity Stone—the Soul Gem. Warlock is a perfect biological specimen whose powers place him among the top echelons of powerful beings in the Multiverse. Warlock also has vast knowledge of, and connections with, the cosmos and its energies. He can harness cosmic energy and manipulate any form of matter. Warlock is also a master of magic thanks to his use of the Soul Gem. He frequently steps in when the universe is under threat and has been a part of the Infinity Watch, an elite group who watch over the Infinity Stones.

MAN-BEAST

13	Vo
Mb	
Man-Beast	

REAL NAME: Unknown **POWERS:** Super-strength; force-field creation; antimatter manipulation; genius intellect **FIRST APPEARANCE:** *Thor* #134 (Nov 1966)

The Man-Beast is created by the High Evolutionary, who wishes to see what happens when he rapidly evolves a wolf. However, the High Evolutionary leaves his machine on for too long, and what results is a combination of a supremely evolved man and wolf. The creature emerges from the laboratory filled with hate, claiming to possess the brain of a man as he would be one million years hence, plus the power of a wolf after the same passage of time. It can sense its opponents' weak points and can construct a psionic force field around itself. Man-Beast almost immediately formulates a plan to evolve more evil New Men like itself in order to subjugate humankind.

NEW MEN

11	Re
Ne	
New Men	

FIRST APPEARANCE: *Thor* #132 (Sep 1966)

The New Men are beings evolved from animals by the High Evolutionary, using his genetics expertise and rapid evolution machine. After they are created, the New Men are taught about the outside world and given training so that they can help defend the High Evolutionary's home on Wundagore Mountain and all the scientific treasures within. Their appearance varies considerably—some clearly resemble upright versions of the animal species they once were, while others can pass for humans, albeit with traits reminiscent of animals. Almost all of the New Men share an advanced intelligence and scientific know-how. They are also devoted to their creator, the High Evolutionary, even though he does not always treat them kindly.

ANCILLARY EXEMPLARS

42	Vo
Ay	
Ayesha	

51	St
Hg	
Higher Evolutionary	

47	Co
Nb	
Nobilus	

Ayesha is created by the same cabal of scientists who create Adam Warlock. Like Adam, the being quickly learns that its creators, known as the Enclave, have evil intentions and leaves them behind. Turning itself into a woman, Ayesha searches the universe for her "brother" Warlock, who is her genetic twin. A restless experimenter, the High Evolutionary also tries to improve on his earlier work by creating the **Higher Evolutionary**— an exact genetic copy of himself with added compassion. Another notable evolutionary anomaly is **Nobilus**, who is created by the High Evolutionary using genetic material harvested from Thor but infused with the essence of the trickster Loki.

QUICKSILVER

REAL NAME: Pietro Maximoff **POWERS:** Super-speed, durability, stamina, reflexes, and agility
FIRST APPEARANCE: *X-Men* #4 (Mar 1964)

Quicksilver's true origins are shrouded in confusion for many years. Long believing that he and his twin, Wanda (aka Scarlet Witch), are the mutant children of Magneto, Quicksilver discovers that he is, in fact, human, but no ordinary one. As a child, he is experimented on by the High Evolutionary and his genes are altered to give him superhuman abilities. He has enhanced strength and superhuman reflexes, agility, durability, and stamina, but what he is most famous for is his super-speed. Quicksilver's physiology is enhanced such that he does not produce fatigue toxins, and his cardiovascular and respiratory systems are enhanced. Able to run at speeds up to 175 mph, Quicksilver is further augmented by the High Evolutionary's Isotope E, increasing his top speed to supersonic levels.

SQUIRREL GIRL

REAL NAME: Doreen Green **POWERS:** Prehensile tail; strong bite; knuckle spike; communication with squirrels; healing factor **FIRST APPEARANCE:** *Marvel Super-Heroes* #8 (Dec 1991)

From birth, Doreen Green is a unique individual. She has a prehensile tail, just like a squirrel, and shares many abilities with that rodent species, such as climbing, an incredibly strong bite, and excellent peripheral vision. When a doctor runs tests on her DNA, Squirrel Girl is proven to be an evolutionary mutate, an example of a *Homo sapiens* with some very unusual genetic anomalies.

Squirrel Girl's ability to communicate with squirrels means that she can use them to help her on missions. This is just one way in which Squirrel Girl approaches missions differently to many heroes. She tries to talk through problems with villains before punching them, and she's claimed some pretty impressive victories over the likes of Galactus and Thanos. Perhaps her methods should be taken seriously.

MANTIS

REAL NAME: Unknown **POWERS:** Emotional sensitivity; telepathy; precognition; pyrokinesis; astral projection **FIRST APPEARANCE:** *Avengers* #112 (Jun 1973)

Mantis starts life as a baseline human, but as a young child, she is taken in by the Priests of Pama, who are secretly Kree scientists, because they believe her to be the prophesied Celestial Madonna. The priests train her to be a superlative martial artist, but they also use their advanced Kree knowledge to endow her with various psionic abilities, including the power to sense the emotions of others.

SCORPION

REAL NAME: Mac Gargan **POWERS:** Super-strength, speed, durability, reflexes, agility; wall-crawling **FIRST APPEARANCE:** *Amazing Spider-Man* #19 (Dec 1964)

Mac Gargan is more than just a man in a scorpion suit. He is actually a mutate— a hybrid of human and scorpion. He is paid by J. Jonah Jameson to take an experimental serum that gives him the proportionate strength of a scorpion. Since the mutation process does not give him a stinging tail of his own, one is built for him as part of his Scorpion costume, which he can control with mental commands. Unfortunately, Gargan is also rendered insane by the process.

CLOAK AND DAGGER

REAL NAMES: Tyrone Johnson; Tandy Bowen **POWERS:** Darkforce shadows; Lightforce blades **FIRST APPEARANCE:** *Peter Parker, The Spectacular Spider-Man* #64 (Mar 1982)

Tyrone Johnson and Tandy Bowen are runaway teens when they are captured for use in an experimental drug test. The substance has a mutagenic effect, giving both individuals opposite yet linked powers. Johnson becomes Cloak, who can harness energy from the Darkforce dimension to create pools of shadow around himself. Bowen, meanwhile, can use the Lightforce to fire blades of energy.

ANCILLARY EXEMPLARS

Kree technology administered by the Lunatic Legion turns Robert Hunter into a mutate in the form of **Nitro**, the living bomb. After exploding, he can gather his atoms and reform. Nitro uses his power to tragic effect in the town of Stamford, Connecticut, triggering the superhuman civil war. Earth-based scientists at A.I.M. turn George Tarleton into **M.O.D.O.K.**, a mutate of such intelligence that his cranium is forced to grow to a giant size to accommodate his brain.

INHUMANS

FIRST APPEARANCE: *Fantastic Four* #45 (Dec 1965)

10	Ba
In	
Inhumans	

The Inhumans, scientific name *Inhomo supremis*, are a race created by the Kree hundreds of thousands of years ago. Kree scientists conduct experiments on early humans to create a race of super-beings that can help them kick-start the Kree's own evolutionary process and also aid them in their seemingly endless war against the Skrull Empire. Although the experiments result in success, and a race of powerful humanoids is created, the Kree abandon them after a prophecy foretells that their creations will destroy their leader, the Supreme Intelligence.

Although the Inhumans are engineered to be superhuman, not all individuals are born with super-powers. For some, their powers are activated only by a process called Terrigenesis, discovered around 25,000 years ago by an Inhuman scientist. When Terrigen Crystals, made from a rare mineral originally created by the Kree, are exposed to a combination of water at a certain temperature, the result is Terrigen Mists. These vapors act as a mutagenic, triggering the abilities of Inhumans when they are exposed to them.

However, sometimes Terrigenesis results in monstrous mutations, so the Inhumans develop a strict genetic testing program overseen by a Genetic Council so that only a few chosen individuals can undergo the process. Terrigenesis is so important to the Inhumans that the Genetic Council that controls it is even more powerful than the monarch.

Thanks to the genetic lineage implanted by the Kree, even Inhumans who do not undergo Terrigenesis tend to have higher levels of strength, stamina, durability, and reflexes than their very distant relatives *Homo sapiens*.

CHOSEN ONES

Controversially, Inhuman king Black Bolt is subjected to the Terrigen Mists while still in the womb. When he is born, he is one of the most powerful Inhumans ever known— a mere whisper of his voice causes a hugely destructive sonic wave. Due to the damage he can cause, he spends most of his life in silence.

Black Bolt's queen is Medusa, whose power resides in her long hair. Medusa can perform feats of great strength or dexterity with her prehensile hair, and even use it as a whiplike weapon. Medusa's sister, Crystal, has elemental powers, while Black Bolt's brother, Maximus, has extensive psionic abilities, although these go hand in hand with mental instability. Other members of the Inhuman Royal Family include Black Bolt's super-strong cousin Gorgon and Black Bolt and Medusa's son, Ahura.

Inhuman scientists also conduct experiments exposing animals to Terrigenesis, one of the results of which is Lockjaw, the beloved pet of the Inhuman Royal Family—a gargantuan dog with the power to teleport. While Inhumans tend to keep to themselves, preferring to remain in their rarefied home of Attilan, sometimes events have conspired to bring them into contact with humans or other species. On one occasion, the two worlds of *Inhomo supremis* and *Homo sapiens* collide dramatically when Black Bolt detonates a Terrigen Bomb on Earth, causing the activation of latent Inhuman genes in many people previously assumed to be baseline human. The individuals empowered as a result of this are termed NuHumans.

MS. MARVEL

NAME: Kamala Khan **POWERS:** Changing size and shape; accelerated healing
FIRST APPEARANCE: *Captain Marvel* #14 (Jul 2013)

Kamala Khan is an ordinary teenager in Jersey City—or so she thinks. When her hometown is covered in Terrigen Mists from a bomb detonated by Inhuman king Black Bolt, Khan discovers that she has latent Inhuman genes. The teenager undergoes the ancient mutagenic process of Terrigenesis inside a Terrigen cocoon right there on the sidewalk. While inside the cocoon, Kamala sees a vision of her favorite Super Heroes, with Captain Marvel (Carol Danvers) front and center.

When Khan emerges from the cocoon, she resembles Danvers in her younger days as Ms. Marvel, although her powers are quite different. Khan is a polymorph, able to stretch her body to great lengths and in various shapes. She can either use her powers across her whole body, becoming entirely giant-size, or focus on isolated parts, for example, making outsize fists. She can also completely alter her appearance to the extent of being able to impersonate someone else.

SELF-DISCOVERY

Although she chooses to keep the name Ms. Marvel, Khan reverts to her natural appearance and devises her own costume. Extensive scientific examination of her powers reveals to Khan that whenever she changes her size, she is borrowing mass from alternate versions of herself in different timelines. At a molecular level, she is time traveling.

While she is still learning about her powers, Ms. Marvel is taken to the home of the Inhumans, where she discovers more about her Inhuman heritage and the process of Terrigenesis that has changed her life so irrevocably.

After undergoing the process of Terrigenesis, teenager Kamala Khan develops the ability to stretch or compress the molecules of her body.

MOON GIRL

REAL NAME: Lunella Lafayette **POWERS:** Swapping consciousnesses; genius intellect **FIRST APPEARANCE:** *Moon Girl and Devil Dinosaur* #1 (Nov 2015)

Thanks to her precocious genius intellect, Lunella Lafayette is one of the few people who knows in advance that she possesses a latent Inhuman gene that might react to the Terrigen Mists covering the world after the detonation of Black Bolt's Terrigen Bomb. Terrified of an unwanted change being forced on her body, Moon Girl, as she is nicknamed by school friends, tries to use her knowledge to avoid Terrigenesis. However, she cannot avoid her transformation and is encased within a cocoon while it takes place. Her new power is to be able to swap consciousnesses with Devil Dinosaur, a mutated, intelligent T-rex who has escaped from an alternate reality.

ULYSSES CAIN

REAL NAME: Ulysses Cain **POWERS:** Precognition; thought projection **FIRST APPEARANCE:** Free Comic Book Day 2016, *Civil War II*, 1 (May 2016)

Ulysses Cain is a college student when his latent Inhuman gene is activated by Black Bolt's Terrigen Bomb. After undergoing Terrigenesis, Cain discovers that he has the ability to see the future. He finds his new power overwhelming and terrifying at first, but it also causes ructions far beyond Ulysses's imagination when one of his visions triggers the second superhuman civil war. Cain's abilities continue to develop as time goes by, and eventually he becomes so powerful that he is invited by Eternity to join the ranks of the cosmic entities. Cain accepts, seizing the chance to no longer be a pawn fought over by squabbling factions of Earth's heroes.

ANCILLARY EXEMPLARS

Daisy Johnson, alias **Quake**, inherits her Inhuman genes from her mother, while her father is villain Mr. Hyde, who alters his own DNA using the Hyde Formula. As a result, Daisy has powers of her own, including the ability to generate vibrations like earthquakes. **Anastasia Kravinoff** also has a villainous lineage mixed with Inhuman genes.

The daughter of Kraven the Hunter inherits his mantle as well as the magical serums that give him superhuman abilities like super-strength, speed, and enhanced senses. Meanwhile, young **Kei Kawade** is affected by the Inhumans' Terrigen Bomb in an oversized way—his latent Inhuman power is to summon monsters simply by drawing them.

INTERSTELLAR ENERGIES

The infinite reaches of the Multiverse offer an equally infinite range of super-powered beings. Some are aliens who are naturally enhanced, while others are beings changed by an encounter with an extraterrestrial phenomenon or artifact.

Cr COSMIC RAYS

Around the Earth are charged radioactive particles that must be negotiated by any craft passing through them. They have a profound effect on the body.

Ge GENETIC ENHANCEMENT

Some individuals benefit from a hybrid alien lineage that boosts their powers well beyond the baseline norm.

Aa ALPHA ALIENS

Many alien species are just naturally stronger or more powerful in some way than humans, making them formidable opponents or valuable allies.

ALPHA ALIENS CONTINUED

45 Vo	43 St	36 Co	17 St	10 Vo	19 Vo
Tn	Br	Bd	Ga	Kr	Sr
Thane	Brood	Badoon	Gamora	Kree	Shi'ar

2 Vo	6 Vo
S	Sp
Skrulls	Super-Skrull

EXTRATERRESTRIAL ENHANCEMENT

In an endless Multiverse, there are all manner of ways in which organisms can be enhanced and upgraded.

18 Ba	22 St	14 Re	35 Vo	44 St
Pq	Nv	Dx	Mi	Dh
Star-Lord	Nova	Drax	Mandarin	Darkhawk

39 St	40 Co	37 St
Sj	Qs	Yu
Starjammers	Quasar	Yondu Udonta

SYMBIOTES

Since Peter Parker inadvertently brought an alien symbiote to Earth, the species and its descendants have bonded with many humans.

23 Re	25 Vo	30 Re
V	Cn	Av
Venom	Carnage	Anti-Venom

31 St
Ft
Agent Venom

RARE SPECIES

While some alien races are extremely numerous, there are others that are much less common and some that may even be wholly unique.

20 St	29 St	16 St
Rr	Gr	Ho
Rocket	Groot	Howard the Duck

24 To	3 Co
Mj	Fm
Mojo	Fin Fang Foom

FANTASTIC FOUR

FIRST APPEARANCE: *Fantastic Four* #1 (Aug 1961)

1   Ba

Ff

Fantastic Four

While many beings get their powers from radiation caused by man-made events like explosions or overdose accidents, the Fantastic Four are unusual in that their superhuman abilities come entirely from naturally occurring radiation—cosmic rays. This radiation comes from charged particles in solar wind that are found in high concentrations in the Van Allen belts around Earth.

The Van Allen belts are held in place by Earth's magnetic field, and they protect the atmosphere beneath them by preventing the radioactive particles from getting closer to the planet's surface. The intensity of the radiation found in these fields is increased greatly by events like solar flares.

Dr. Reed Richards, Ben Grimm, and siblings Susan and Johnny Storm come into contact with the Van Allen belts while on a test flight of a spacecraft designed by Richards. Although the ship is shielded from cosmic rays, the radiation intensity is higher than expected, and the four humans are bombarded by the rays. Forced to abort their exploratory mission and return to Earth, they discover that the cosmic rays have had a mutagenic effect on their bodies, and they now possess strange new abilities.

Richards can render his entire body malleable, stretching or compressing it into any shape. His friend Ben Grimm becomes a super-strong being with a rocklike appearance, but his transformation is more than just skin-deep. Every physical aspect of his body is made tougher, right through to muscles, organs, and the skeletal structure. After exposure to the cosmic rays, Sue Storm soon realizes she can now become invisible by mentally redirecting light rays around her body, although the full extent of her powers is revealed gradually. She can also

create force fields for defense or for directing at opponents as shock waves. Her brother, Johnny, meanwhile, is able to transform his body into flaming plasma as well as conjure shapes from fire. As a consequence of the high levels of hydrogen in his fiery state, Johnny can also become buoyant and fly by shooting out jets of flame behind him.

FAMILY FIRST

Although their new powers are a lot to deal with, the Fantastic Four take the decision to stick together as a team and use their abilities to help people. Reed Richards also continues to use his genius intellect in every way he can to equip the team with everything they need for their new lives as the first family of Super Heroes. His flair for invention and discovery is undimmed by their brush with cosmic rays. Science is one of the crucial pillars supporting the Fantastic Four, but equally important is the concept of family. The team support each other, bicker frequently, and share an unbreakable bond.

CAPTAIN MARVEL

13	Ba

Cm

Captain Marvel

REAL NAME: Carol Danvers **POWERS:** Durability; energy manipulation; flight; healing factor; "seventh" sense of danger
FIRST APPEARANCE: *Marvel Super-Heroes* #13 (Mar 1968)

Carol Danvers is an ordinary, albeit high-achieving, human—or so she believes. Working as head of security at NASA, she becomes caught up in a clash between the Kree hero Captain Marvel (Mar-Vell) and Kree Commander Yon-Rogg. In the melee, Danvers is struck by radiation from an exploding Kree device, the Psyche-Magnitron. Later, she realizes that not only has she survived the accident, but she also has been given incredible powers typical of those associated with the alien Kree. For many years, it is assumed that her powers are a replication of Mar-Vell's—because the radiation passes through his body before striking Danvers—but the truth is that Kree abilities have lain dormant in her genes since birth. Unbeknownst to Danvers, her mother is a former Kree warrior who retires to Earth to raise her daughter as a human. The Psyche-Magnitron blast is the trigger that awakens Danvers's buried Kree genetic heritage.

The alien Kree abilities now manifest in Danvers are truly extraordinary, instantly making her one of the most formidable Super Heroes on the planet. As well as super-strength, speed, durability, and flight, she also has a very useful "seventh sense" that alerts her when she is in danger from attack. Later, Danvers loses her powers, and even her memories, during an encounter with the mutant Rogue. Although her memories are restored, her emotional ties to them are not, and so, feeling isolated, she leaves Earth behind to explore space. An encounter with the scientists of the extraterrestrial Brood leads to her lost genetic abilities being replaced with the power of a white hole. She then takes on the new identity of Binary.

Danvers is now able to channel the energy of a star into blasts from her hands or eyes, fly, and survive the harshest conditions of deep space. Although she later sacrifices her permanent Binary powers to save Earth's sun from dying, Danvers is still able to summon them for short periods if she absorbs a sufficient amount of energy. In this form, she is the most powerful version of herself.

PRICE OF POWER

However, Danvers's great power does not come without a cost, and, from the outset, she struggles with her genetic inheritance. Early on, she even blacks out when using her powers and then has no recollection of them when she reverts to her civilian identity. Eventually, she reconciles her two identities, learning to live as both Carol Danvers and the Super Hero Ms. Marvel—although she later adopts her old friend's "Captain Marvel" moniker in his honor. On her tough, heroic journey, Carol Danvers is knocked down many times by abuse, addiction issues, and amnesia. But she always picks herself up and carries on thanks, to her indomitable willpower—a fundamental attribute she has possessed for much longer than her cosmic super-powers.

CAPTAIN MARVEL (MAR-VELL)

REAL NAME: Mar-Vell **POWERS:** Enhanced Kree super-powers; resistance to toxins; flight; cosmic awareness **FIRST APPEARANCE:** *Marvel Super-Heroes* #12 (Dec 1967)

11   St

Mv

Captain Marvel
(Mar-Vell)

The first Captain Marvel is the Kree warrior known as Mar-Vell. Like all Kree, Mar-Vell is naturally stronger, faster, and more durable than Earth's humans and has greater resistance to toxins and disease. Energy absorption and manipulation enables him to fly, fire energy blasts, and heal rapidly. At first, he uses equipment—Kree Nega-Bands—to do this, but later he learns that he can achieve his energy powers himself. Mar-Vell is further boosted by the alien Zo, who increases his strength and enables him to move faster than light, effectively teleporting. Later, his powers are enhanced again by the cosmic entity Eon, with the aim of making him capable of defeating the Mad Titan Thanos. Despite his immunity to disease, Mar-Vell eventually dies after succumbing to a form of cancer contracted from exposure to nerve gas.

GENIS-VELL

REAL NAME: Genis-Vell **POWERS:** Super-strength, durability, reflexes; flight; stellar energy absorption; cosmic awareness **FIRST APPEARANCE:** *Silver Surfer Annual* #6 (Oct 1993)

26   Vo

Gv

Photon

Genis-Vell, aka Photon, inherits incredible powers from both his parents: Mar-Vell, an enhanced Kree warrior, and Elysius, a being created using DNA from the Eternals. His superior genetics give him incredible strength, speed, stamina, durability, agility, and reflexes, plus the ability to harness stellar energy to boost his powers still further. He can also enhance his abilities by using Nega-Bands inherited from his father. Genis-Vell's cosmic awareness feeds him information not available to regular senses, such as the potential outcomes of his actions. However, the bombardment of images from every possible future causes acute mental instability. Genis-Vell even destroys and remakes the universe before being killed by Baron Zemo to prevent him from threatening existence itself.

PHYLA-VELL

REAL NAME: Phyla-Vell **POWERS:** Super-strength; energy absorption via Nega-Bands and Quantum Bands; energy constructs **FIRST APPEARANCE:** *Captain Marvel* #16 (Jan 2004)

27	St
Pv	
Phyla-Vell	

Phyla-Vell is the sister of Genis-Vell, and, like him, she inherits both enhanced Kree and Eternals DNA from her biological parents, Mar-Vell and Elysius. However, her hybrid genetics make her far more powerful than either of her parents.

Like her father and brother, Phyla boosts her already impressive genetic abilities by channeling energy from the Negative Zone using Nega-Bands. These are superseded and absorbed by the unique Quantum Bands, which Phyla later uses in a similar way, accessing energy from the Quantum Zone. She can use these bands to make energy constructs, one of which is a weapon called the Quantum Sword. Later, she becomes an avatar of the cosmic being Oblivion and is killed with her own sword by Magus—an evil future version of Adam Warlock.

HULKLING

REAL NAME: Teddy Altman **POWERS:** Super-strength, stamina, durability; shape-shifting, including wings for flight; healing factor **FIRST APPEARANCE:** *Young Avengers* #1 (Apr 2005)

28	St
Hk	
Hulkling	

Teddy Altman is a genetic hybrid of two powerful alien races: the Kree and the Skrulls. Tragically, he is born at a time when the two races are embroiled in a long and bitter war. His father is the enhanced Kree hero Mar-Vell and his

mother is a Skrull princess who sends Altman to Earth as she fears that his mixed heritage will endanger him on the Skrull Throneworld. Altman has strength levels above those of baseline Kree, both due to his Skrull ancestry and because his father was already genetically enhanced above regular Kree. He has also inherited the keystone Skrull ability of shape-shifting, which he uses most commonly to assume a form resembling a young Hulk. This also inspires his name, Hulkling, though Altman has no gamma-related abilities like the original Hulk.

CELESTIALS

POWERS: Super-strength; invulnerability; cosmic powers; omnipotence; life-creating powers
FIRST APPEARANCE: *Eternals* #1 (Jul 1976)

21	St
Cl	
Celestials	

There are few beings in the cosmos more powerful than the Celestials. Thousands of feet tall, each Celestial wears colorful armor and a helmet. It is hard for lesser beings like humans to understand the Celestials' physiology and motivations, so they use the simplistic sobriquet "Space Gods." The truth is a little more complex. Celestials appear to be bio-mechanical in nature. They take a scientific interest in the evolution of life, experimenting on the species they find and monitoring their development. Every millennium, they return to a planet for 50 years to judge whether a species deserves to continue. If it is deemed unworthy, it is culled. The Celestials are generally dispassionate observers, but occasionally, an individual's interest in a planet grows into a form of affection.

ELDERS

POWERS: Wielding the Power Primordial in various ways to achieve mental or physical superiority in a particular facet of their lives **FIRST APPEARANCE:** *Avengers* #28 (May 1966)

8	Vo
El	
Elders	

The Elders of the Universe are ancient and extremely powerful entities who all possess a fragment of the Power Primordial and have learned to control and wield it. The Power Primordial is the interstellar energy left over from the Big Bang. Each Elder has a different form of this power, and each individual is the last surviving member of his or her species. Although they also have other names, Elders tend to be known by a name that summarizes their main interest, for example, the Collector. Another Elder, the Grandmaster, loves to play games. He is so powerful that he is able to assemble a lineup of the strongest Super Heroes from Earth to fight each other, simply for his amusement. Other key Elders include the Gardener, the Champion, and the Astronomer.

BUILDERS

33	Vo
Bu	
Builders	

POWERS: Shaping the structure of space and time; destroying worlds; enabling species' higher evolution
FIRST APPEARANCE: *Avengers* #2 (Feb 2013)

The Builders are the oldest living things in the universe and they can be classified into two types: Creators and Engineers. They are created by Captain Universe— the manifestation of the Uni-Power and the protector of all life—whom at first they worship as a mother goddess. As the universe expands, the Builders devise aggressive systems to control space and time. To this end, they create Gardeners to roam the universe and destroy any worlds deemed unfit for existence. The Builders are exceedingly powerful, evidenced by the fact that just one individual is able to destroy an Annihilation Wave by merely "tweaking" its invading creatures so that they devour each other instead of attacking the Builders.

EX NIHILO

32	Vo
Ex	
Ex Nihilo	

NAME: Ex Nihilo **POWERS:** Creating and controlling plant life; altering genetics of organisms; energy blasts; longevity
FIRST APPEARANCE: *Avengers* #1 (Feb 2013)

Ex Nihilo is a Gardener—a being created by the Builders to seed new life throughout the universe to encourage species to evolve into higher forms. However, he also has the power to end life if he judges it unworthy of existence. Along with his sister, Abyss, Ex Nihilo is born from a seed carried by an Aleph—robotic beings designed by the Builders to purge unfit worlds. When the two are on Mars, they use their life-building interstellar energies to create verdant plant life on the red planet. The siblings then start creating "perfect" versions of the humans that inhabit the nearest planet.

WATCHERS

4	St
Wa	
Watchers	

POWERS: Almost limitless cosmic powers, including manipulation of time, space, and matter **FIRST APPEARANCE:** *Fantastic Four* #13 (Apr 1963)

The Watchers have existed since just after the dawn of the Multiverse. Naturally omnipotent beings, they have almost limitless cosmic power. Possessing extreme mental abilities, they can manipulate time, space, energy, and matter at a molecular level. Nevertheless, they rarely use these extensive powers. Ever since the actions of a Watcher once led to the destruction of a planet, they have kept to a strict observational role, recording events but not influencing them. However, the Watcher named Uatu, who is stationed on Earth's moon, has been known to overstep his allotted role, interceding when humanity is threatened. He is even put on trial for this breach, but it doesn't stop him. Uatu is later deemed to have committed this misdemeanor hundreds of times.

GALACTUS

REAL NAME: Galan **POWERS:** Power Cosmic; immortality; omnipotence; molecular control; energy absorption; colossal energy blasts **FIRST APPEARANCE:** *Fantastic Four* #48 (Mar 1966)

7	St
Gc	
Galactus	

Galactus is an awesome being in the truest sense of the word. A vast, towering figure of almost limitless power, he is feared throughout the universe. The terror Galactus invokes is justified because he exists by consuming energy—specifically the life energy of a star or planet—and he cares little about the consequences for the species that inhabit those worlds. The mighty Galactus is the sole survivor of the universe that is destroyed in the Big Bang, and he exists in a form of stasis until the fledgling universe has expanded enough to support his insatiable appetite. He is the chief wielder of the Power Cosmic— an interstellar energy that provides him with seemingly endless godlike powers.

ALL-CONSUMING POWERS

Galactus does not always operate alone. He is usually accompanied by a herald— a series of beings whom he imbues with the Power Cosmic and sends out to find suitable worlds for him to consume. When Galactus arrives at the unfortunate world that he has selected for his next meal,

he constructs a giant machine on its surface for the purpose of efficiently extracting the energy on which he feeds. Unless he gets sufficient nourishment, Galactus's great powers can rapidly grow weaker and he would eventually die.

Following the restoration of the Multiverse after it is destroyed in the Incursions, a group of heroes manage to solve the perennial problem of Galactus's hunger. They remake Galactus as a Lifebringer so he is now free of his need to consume worlds and is instead focused on restoring to existence the planets he has previously eaten.

Known as the Devourer of Worlds, Galactus's power depends on his ability to "eat" entire worlds, including Earth, which has, so far, evaded consumption.

SILVER SURFER

REAL NAME: Norrin Radd **POWERS:** Power Cosmic; can absorb, manipulate, and discharge energy across electromagnetic spectrum **FIRST APPEARANCE:** *Fantastic Four* #48 (Mar 1966)

5	Re
Ss	
Silver Surfer	

Norrin Radd becomes the Silver Surfer when he offers himself as Galactus's herald in exchange for the Devourer of Worlds sparing his home planet, Zenn-La. The Silver Surfer is already genetically advanced, coming from a long-lived and technologically progressive race. But Galactus imbues the Silver Surfer with a fragment of the Power Cosmic, which even in a small quantity enhances his body and makes him extraordinarily powerful. Thanks to Galactus, the Silver Surfer's skin turns into a silver, near-indestructible material. As herald, the Surfer's job is to scout ahead of his master looking for suitable planets for him to consume. He generally tries to find uninhabited worlds, but this is not always possible and it becomes increasingly difficult over time. Galactus alters the Silver Surfer's brain, dampening his guilt response so that he is not endlessly tormented by the lives lost as a result of his actions. Despite this, however, the Silver Surfer does form a special attachment to Earth and helps prevent Galactus from destroying it. He has great admiration for humans, despite also feeling great frustration at their capacity for mindless violence.

ANCILLARY EXEMPLARS

42	St
Aw	
Air-Walker	

38	Vo
Fl	
Firelord	

41	Vo
Tx	
Terrax	

Although the Silver Surfer is the best known and perhaps most powerful of those beings selected to wield the Power Cosmic as a herald of Galactus, he is by no means the only one. The Surfer's replacement is **Air-Walker**, a former member of the Nova Corps. Galactus becomes so attached to him that when he is killed, the Devourer of Worlds creates a robot body so that the Air-Walker's consciousness can live on. He is replaced by **Firelord**, a former Nova Corps comrade, who does not serve for long before being freed by Thor. Later, **Terrax the Tamer** is Galactus's herald. He is chosen because he is less principled than his predecessors, which Galactus hopes will mean he will get to consume more worlds. Terrax's innate earth-moving powers are significantly increased by the Power Cosmic.

THANOS

REAL NAME: Thanos **POWERS:** Super-strength, speed, durability, agility, and reflexes; immunity to toxins; immortality; genius intellect **FIRST APPEARANCE:** *Iron Man* #55 (Feb 1973)

15	Co

T

Thanos

Thanos is an Eternal born on Titan, but he has a different appearance to other Eternals due to having Deviant Syndrome. This manifests in the form of purple skin and an oversized body, making Thanos outwardly resemble a Deviant more than an Eternal. His strength levels exceed those of other Eternals, and he can increase his strength by harnessing interstellar energy, which he can then fire out in powerful blasts. Thanos is not just a powerhouse—he has a genius intellect, particularly in the fields of science and invention, and also possesses psionic abilities like telepathy.

As a young man, he becomes obsessed with death, developing a taste for killing and also falling in love with the physical manifestation of Death, who appears to him in the form of a young woman. From then onward, Thanos devotes his long life and his prodigious powers to trying to win the heart of his capricious mistress through conquest and mass slaughter. She repays his loyalty by resurrecting him when he is killed, making him effectively immortal.

INFINITY AWAITS

Although he is already naturally very powerful, Thanos embarks on a quest to collect the six Infinity Gems in order to extend his dominion still further. After successfully gathering the Gems, Thanos becomes virtually omnipotent, but he is eventually defeated by a coalition that includes Adam Warlock and his own granddaughter, Nebula. Thanos is frequently deemed an ever-present danger to the universe, but sometimes he surprisingly allies with heroic individuals and teams against all-powerful beings who pose an even greater existential threat.

Thanos is capable of manipulating and controling cosmic energy to project devastating blasts from his hands and infrared heat beams from his eyes.

BLACK ORDER

34	Vo
Bk	
Black Order	

POWERS: Various deadly powers, used in the service of Thanos the Mad Titan **FIRST APPEARANCE:** *New Avengers* #8 (Sep 2013)

Also known as the Cull Obsidian, the Black Order is a ruthless team of five who serve Thanos. Super-strong Corvus Glaive gets immortality from a blade. His wife, Proxima Midnight, harnesses the powers of a star, supernova, and black hole. Black Dwarf has impenetrable skin. Ebony Maw can bend minds to his will, and Supergiant is an unstable telepath.

BLASTAAR

9	Vo
Bl	
Blastaar	

REAL NAME: Blastaar **POWERS:** Super-strength, speed, durability, agility, and reflexes; concussive blasts **FIRST APPEARANCE:** *Fantastic Four* #62 (May 1967)

Blastaar is a super-strong tyrannical ruler from the planet Baluur in the Negative Zone. His hunger for territory brings him into conflict with the Zone's other heavy hitter, Annihilus. Blastaar manages to take his rival's powerful Cosmic Control Rod, but not for long. Without it, Blastaar has to rely on his brute strength, talent for intimidation, and concussive blasts.
His blasts appear to be a natural ability, which he uses against other beings and structures, and to propel himself through the air in a form of flight.

ANNIHILUS

12	Vo
Ah	
Annihilus	

REAL NAME: Annihilus **POWERS:** Cosmic Control Rod gives powers; flight; resurrection **FIRST APPEARANCE:** *Fantastic Four Annual* #6 (Nov 1968)

Annihilus is a highly evolved insectoid alien from the Negative Zone. His phobia of dying causes him to seek out and destroy any potential threat. He is aided in his war against death by the Cosmic Control Rod—an artifact so powerful, it puts Annihilus on a level with exceptional beings like Thanos. He also commands a vast armada called the Annihilation Wave.

ANCILLARY EXEMPLARS

45	Vo
Tn	
Thane	

43	St
Br	
Brood	

36	Co
Bd	
Badoon	

Of the many hugely potent aliens in the universe, one who has inherited a terrible legacy is **Thane**, son of Thanos. He has Inhuman genes from his mother as well as a "death touch" that he struggles to control. There are also entire races instinctively bent on conquest, like the **Brood**— predatory insectoids trying to spawn themselves across the universe, and reveling in others' suffering. Another is the **Badoon**—barbaric, reptilian allies of Thanos—most notable for their strictly separated gender-based societies.

GAMORA

REAL NAME: Gamora **POWERS:** Technological upgrades to skeleton and respiratory system; advanced combat skills; healing factor **FIRST APPEARANCE:** *Strange Tales* #180 (Jun 1975)

Gamora's natural alien strength, speed, and stamina are enhanced with intense training and technological alterations. Originally from the Earth-7528 reality, she is brought to the 616 universe by Thanos as the last survivor of her race, the Zen-Whoberis. Her upbringing is far from the peace-loving ways of her people, as Thanos trains her until she is the deadliest woman in the galaxy. His aim is to make Gamora his weapon against the Magus—an evil future version of Adam Warlock. The Mad Titan also uses technology to give her a new skeletal structure in a lightweight alloy that is virtually indestructible, as well as enhanced reflexes and a new respiratory system. Gamora also has her powers temporarily but massively enhanced by the Black Vortex and the Infinity Gems.

KREE

POWERS: Super-strength (twice the baseline level of a human); dense bodies; mind powers occasionally possessed by female Kree **FIRST APPEARANCE:** *Fantastic Four* #65 (Aug 1967)

The Kree are a scientifically interesting race because their history is shaped by their evolution—or lack of it. They are an evolutionary dead-end at risk of being left behind by other races. The Kree ruler, the Supreme Intelligence, kick-starts the Kree revival with a drastic act—he coerces the Kree's enemies, the Shi'ar, into using a deadly Nega-Bomb on the Kree. While 98 percent of Kree die, the survivors are those with the genetic ability to deal with the bomb's radiation. These strong, adaptive individuals strengthen the Kree bloodline. Kree are about twice as strong as Earth humans and have denser bodies—due in part to their environment having stronger gravity and air with less oxygen and more nitrogen. Originally Kree have blue skin, but over time a new pink-skinned variant appears.

SHI'AR

19	Vo
Sr	
Shi'ar	

POWERS: Some but not all Shi'ar individuals manifest super-powers; others have wings **FIRST APPEARANCE:** *X-Men* #97 (Feb 1976)

Although humanoid in appearance, the birdlike alien Shi'ar still bear the vestigial traces of their avian ancestors, with feathered heads and hollow bones. Some Shi'ar even have wings, but they are genetic throwbacks regarded as mutants. The Shi'ar are scientifically minded and natural voyagers, although they are not a pacific people. Instead, they use their talents to amass a vast empire. Their expansionism brings them into contact with other dominant alien civilizations such as the Kree and the Skrulls. Like humans, some but not all Shi'ar manifest super-powers, and it is from this pool of super-powered individuals that the Shi'ar elite Imperial Guard is formed.

SKRULLS

2	Vo
S	
Skrulls	

POWERS: Shape-shifting; flight, if they assume a shape with wings **FIRST APPEARANCE:** *Fantastic Four* #2 (Sep 1961)

Like humans on Earth, the reptilian Skrull race is visited long ago by Celestials and experimented on. This genetic tampering produces Eternal Skrulls, baseline Skrulls, and Deviant Skrulls. Unlike their equivalents on Earth, the Deviant Skrulls exterminate their brethren and become the only extant version of their species. These green-skinned Skrulls rise to form a vast galactic empire and fight endless wars against other extraterrestrial conquerors. Skrulls naturally possess the ability to shape-shift into any form, imitating other beings with uncanny accuracy. They can also fly by reshaping their bodies to "grow" wings.

SUPER-SKRULL

6	Vo
Sp	
Super-Skrull	

REAL NAME: Kl'rt **POWERS:** Enhanced shape-shifting **FIRST APPEARANCE:** *Fantastic Four* #18 (Sep 1963)

Kl'rt is a hardened Skrull warrior who is then genetically engineered to manifest the powers of each member of the Fantastic Four. He is the first beneficiary of the new Super-Skrull program—a technological procedure to augment Skrulls. Receptors are implanted in his body that are capable of harnessing the same cosmic radiation that gives the Fantastic Four their powers. Kl'rt also has the advantage of being able to use more than one of these powers simultaneously. And thanks to the genes that allow Skrulls to shape-shift, Kl'rt can also take on the appearance of any of the Fantastic Four while he is mimicking their powers.

Following the success of the Super-Skrull process on Kl'rt, many more Skrulls are similarly empowered with the abilities of different Earth Super Heroes.

STAR-LORD

REAL NAME: Peter Quill **POWERS:** Channeling divine energy through his Element Gun
FIRST APPEARANCE: *Marvel Preview* #4 (Jan 1976)

18	Ba
Pq	
Star-Lord	

Peter Quill is a genetic hybrid: half-human and half-Spartax. The Spartax, of whom his father was emperor, are an alien race with far greater longevity than humans. Quill is left on Earth with his mother, but she is later killed by aliens seeking to end the royal bloodline of Spartax. Quill manages to fight off the extraterrestrials, discovering in the process a mysterious gun that apparently came from his father. Quill has a desire to explore space, and he takes the opportunity as soon as he can by stealing a Kree spacecraft that has come into NASA's possession.

FINDING HIMSELF

At first Quill's space adventures take the form of piracy, but he later finds himself in the role of military consultant to the Kree Empire. He then forms the Guardians of the Galaxy team in response to the major threats posed by the Annihilation Wave and the Phalanx. Quill is apparently killed in battle against the evil gods of New Olympus, but in reality, he has been taken to a different universe. Here, he discovers that his Element Gun has absorbed a vast amount of divine energy from the Olympians. More than a century passes in Quill's new home, but this period is only a few months in his home reality. When he chooses to return to his original universe to save his adopted one, a vision of the Master of the Sun appears to him. It tells Quill that he will be made a true Star-Lord and he will be able to channel vast amounts of energy through his new and improved Element Gun.

Star-Lord's Element Gun draws on the powers of the four elements. It does not diminish with use, and it can find its way into his hands when he calls.

NOVA

22	St
Nv	
Nova	

REAL NAME: Richard Rider **POWERS:** Flight; energy blasts; healing factor; connection to Xandarian Worldmind **FIRST APPEARANCE:** *Nova* #1 (Sep 1976)

Earthman Richard Rider is chosen to be the Nova Prime—the lead warrior of the Nova Corps. This gives him access to the powerful Nova Force and a host of superhuman abilities. He is able to fly, has extraordinary levels of strength, and can harness and fire Nova Force energy. He is also linked to the Worldmind, a computer repository of the accumulated knowledge of the people of Xandar, who are the traditional keepers of the Nova Force. After Xandar and virtually the entire Nova Corps is wiped out by the Annihilation Wave, Rider possesses nearly all the Nova Force himself, which raises his power levels significantly.

DRAX

14	Re
Dx	
Drax	

REAL NAME: Arthur Douglas **POWERS:** Super-strength, stamina, durability, and senses; healing factor **FIRST APPEARANCE:** *Iron Man* #55 (Feb 1973)

Drax the Destroyer has a curious and unique biological pedigree. He is created using the soul of a deceased Earth human, Arthur Douglas. The soul is placed into a new body created by Kronos and Mentor—the grandfather and father of Thanos. Now called Drax, this being is designed with the express purpose of destroying Thanos. Although his main purpose in life is destruction, Drax is deemed to be an Avatar of Life because of the means by which he is created. At first, his new body is large and extremely strong, but after he is killed, he is resurrected in a smaller, weaker body, albeit with greater intelligence.

ANCILLARY EXEMPLARS

35	Vo
Mi	
Mandarin	

44	St
Dh	
Darkhawk	

40	Co
Qs	
Quasar	

39	St
Sj	
Starjammers	

37	St
Yu	
Yondu Udonta	

There are many ways in which organisms can be enhanced. The villain the **Mandarin** acquires powers from a set of ring-shaped artifacts. Chris Powell uses an ancient Shi'ar amulet to fight for good as **Darkhawk**. Shi'ar technology is also used by the piratical **Starjammers** to strike back at an oppressive empire. The Quantum Bands turn Wendell Vaughn and his successors into the powerful energy being **Quasar**. Meanwhile, **Yondu Udonta** has perfect control over a lethal arrow made from the Centaurian metal yaka, which responds to sounds.

VENOM

REAL NAME: Eddie Brock **POWERS:** After bonding with a host, the symbiote picks up any and all of the host's powers **FIRST APPEARANCE:** *Amazing Spider-Man* #299 (Apr 1988)

23   Re

V

Venom

Venom is the name taken on Earth by a particular alien symbiote when it bonds with Eddie Brock. The symbiote is created, along with many others of its kind, by an all-powerful dark god named Knull. He wants revenge on the Celestials for bringing light into the universe. The nature of the relationship this symbiote has with its hosts leads it to become heavily influenced by the personality type of whoever it bonds with. However, its fundamental instinct is good—to protect its host, whoever they may be. This usually causes the symbiote to transform them into a terrifying monster. However, it can also assume the appearance of a normal human in clothes, if blending in is required.

SPIDER VENOM

One of the first humans the symbiote bonds with is Peter Parker (Spider-Man). He has an enormous influence on the symbiote from then on, even bestowing Spider-Man's powers on all its subsequent hosts. While it views

Spider-Man as its ideal host, Spidey's rejection of their bond fills it with fury—a fury that it unleashes in partnership with its next host, disgraced journalist Eddie Brock. Together, they become Venom. Thanks to the symbiote, Brock knows Spider-Man's secret identity, so he can target Spidey's friends and family.

The symbiote often chooses to leave Eddie and seek out other hosts. It makes no secret of its disappointment with some hosts and often seeks out a stronger individual. Although it can seem irredeemably corrupted, the symbiote has also tried to overcome its feelings of rage and seek some form of redemption.

The symbiote bonds with Peter Parker and imprints the hero's spider-powers onto itself before making Spider-Man's enemy, Eddie Brock, its new host.

CARNAGE

REAL NAME: Cletus Kasady **POWERS:** Spider-powers from Venom; shape-shifting **FIRST APPEARANCE:** *Amazing Spider-Man* #360 (Mar 1992)

Carnage is the twisted combination of Venom's offspring and human serial killer Cletus Kasady. The union of Cletus's sociopathic tendencies with the extraordinary spider-powers inherited from the symbiote's parent gives Carnage greater strength than either Spider-Man or Venom. Although Kasady and this symbiote are separated many times, the symbiote always seeks the same host out. Even after the two are parted more permanently when the symbiote is consumed by Venom, traces of the symbiote remain in Kasady's bloodstream. This enables the human to recreate and bond with a new version of the symbiote.

ANTI-VENOM

REAL NAME: Eddie Brock **POWERS:** Spider-powers and the negation of them in others; matter manipulation **FIRST APPEARANCE:** *Amazing Spider-Man* #569 (Oct 2008)

When fragments of the Venom symbiote in former host Eddie Brock's bloodstream merge with white blood cells, the result is Anti-Venom. This reaction is triggered when Mister Negative uses the Lightforce to cure Brock of cancer. When the original symbiote tries to bond with Brock again, it discovers that Brock is now toxic to it. Although as Anti-Venom Brock regains all the spider-powers he had as Venom, paradoxically he also seems to have a dampening effect on the spider-powers of others near him. This new ability is very useful when a virus infects the entire population of Manhattan with spider-powers. Anti-Venom is able to reverse the effects and become the hero of the hour.

AGENT VENOM

REAL NAME: Flash Thompson **POWERS:** Spider-powers from Venom; shape-shifting; healing factor **FIRST APPEARANCE:** *Amazing Spider-Man* #654 (Apr 2011)

Agent Venom is created as part of Project Rebirth 2.0—an updated version of the Super-Soldier Program using symbiotes. The first successful subject is Flash Thompson, who is a wounded war veteran and former classmate of Peter Parker. After Thompson is bonded with the Venom symbiote, he is able to regrow his legs that were lost in combat, and he acquires all the powers of his hero Spider-Man. He is given drugs to help dampen the symbiote's bloodlust, although this is not fully effective. After taking on missions for the US government, Agent Venom travels into space with the Guardians of the Galaxy, where he learns more about the symbiote's extraterrestrial origins. The symbiote, for its part, regards Thompson as one of its favorite hosts.

ROCKET

REAL NAME: Rocket Raccoon **POWERS:** Senses equivalent to an Earth raccoon; strength, durability, and reflexes; high intelligence **FIRST APPEARANCE:** *Marvel Preview* #7 (Jun 1976)

20	St
Rr	
Rocket	

Species do not come much rarer than Rocket Raccoon. Born on Halfworld—a giant asylum for the mentally troubled—he is bred as a therapy animal for the inmates. However, soon the scientists leave and their robot assistants don't want to look after the patients either, so they genetically evolve the animals to do the job. Rocket undergoes painful procedures until he loses his "softness." He is now a bipedal, talking raccoon with advanced intelligence and cybernetic enhancements, but he retains his naturally heightened raccoon senses. After leaving Halfworld and having adventures with the Guardians of the Galaxy, Rocket realizes that his body has begun to reject its modifications. He has to go through weeks of surgeries to replace his old bio-modifications, but his life is saved.

GROOT

REAL NAME: Groot **POWERS:** Durability; elasticity; healing factor; fluorescent spore production; genius intellect **FIRST APPEARANCE:** *Tales to Astonish* #13 (Nov 1960)

29	St
Gr	
Groot	

Groot is one of an unusual species known as *Flora colossi*, native to Planet X. Treelike beings, the *Flora colossi* grow immensely large and strong, and they absorb knowledge photosynthetically via sunlight. Because their larynxes are made of wood, it seems to many that their speech is limited to, "I am Groot." However, *Flora colossi* are capable of complex communication, and those who know them well can learn their language. Groot's apparent lack of vocabulary can mislead others into thinking he is a simple being, but in fact all of his species are hugely intelligent. Amazingly, *Flora colossi* can regrow their entire bodies from a tiny fragment, so they are able to survive almost any injury. They can also change size and temporarily "stretch" parts of themselves with rapid growth.

HOWARD THE DUCK

16   St
Ho
Howard the
Duck

REAL NAME: Howard Duckson **POWERS:** Master of Quack Fu; enhanced reflexes; indomitable willpower
FIRST APPEARANCE: *Fear* #19 (Dec 1973)

Howard the Duck comes from the reality of Earth-791021. He is a native of Duckworld, a planet that strongly resembles Earth-616 except for the fact that its dominant species is an evolved form of water fowl. Howard stands out on his native world as an individual unsatisfied with a humdrum life and restless to explore beyond his immediate horizons. Howard gets that chance when the Cosmic Axis plucks him from Duckworld and places him in Cleveland, Ohio. Here, he must learn to live as the ultimate outsider, but he is helped by his human girlfriend, Beverly.

MOJO

24   To
Mj
Mojo

REAL NAME: Mojo **POWERS:** Mystical energy bolts; mind control; emits anti-life field outside the Mojoverse
FIRST APPEARANCE: *Longshot* #3 (Nov 1985)

Mojo is the ruler of the planet and pocket dimension named after him—Mojoworld in the Mojoverse. A yellow-skinned Spineless One, he is unable to get around without a robotic hoverchair. A powerful sorceror, Mojo maintains a tyrannical hold over his subjects by giving them a constant supply of entertaining TV

shows. He discovers that Earth's X-Men are ratings winners, so he clashes with the heroes many times while attempting to capture their adventures for his audiences. He and his devoted workers have an excellent command of technological innovation, but they mostly use it to improve their TV shows.

FIN FANG FOOM

3   Co
Fm
Fin Fang Foom

REAL NAME: Unknown **POWERS:** Longevity; shape-shifting; energy absorption; fire breath; telepathy
FIRST APPEARANCE: *Strange Tales* #89 (Oct 1961)

Although the reptilian creature known as Fin Fang Foom resembles a dragon of legend, he is actually an alien Makluan who crash-landed on Earth. His species is extraordinarily long-lived, and he remains on Earth for hundreds of years, frequently in a state of slumber. His giant size and his combustible breath might make it tempting to categorize him simply as a monster, but Fin Fang Foom is a complex, intelligent being and he has on more than one occasion shown signs of just wanting a peaceful existence.

Fin Fang Foom's spirit is able to live on after his body dies and finds itself a new host. He combines different lizard species from Earth to make himself a new body, which means his DNA is now of mixed alien and Earth origin. Scientific analysis of Fin Fang Foom also reveals traces of human genes, although it is unknown how they came to be there.

1	Dr. Reed Richards	14	Watchers	28	Kree	42	Anti-Venom
2	Susan Storm	15	Galactus	29	Shi'ar	43	Agent Venom
3	Ben Grimm	16	Silver Surfer	30	Skrulls	44	Rocket
4	Johnny Storm	17	Air-Walker	31	Super-Skrull	45	Groot
5	Captain Marvel	18	Firelord	32	Star-Lord	46	Howard the Duck
6	Captain Marvel (Mar-Vell)	19	Terrax	33	Nova	47	Mojo
7	Genis-Vell	20	Thanos	34	Drax	48	Fin Fang Foom
8	Phyla-Vell	21	Black Order	35	Mandarin		
9	Hulkling	22	Blastaar	36	Darkhawk		
10	Celestials	23	Annihilus	37	Starjammers		
11	Elders	24	Thane	38	Quasar		
12	Builders	25	Brood	39	Yondu Udonta		
13	Ex Nihilo	26	Badoon	40	Venom		
		27	Gamora	41	Carnage		

85

CHEMICAL REACTIONS

There is no end of geniuses in the field of science, pushing humans to the peak of their potential. But chemistry can be a dangerous vocation, and unpredictable reactions can change lives forever. In the lab, there is a fine line between superhuman and monster.

Ss SUPER-SOLDIER SERUM

The seemingly irreproducible feat of creating Captain America using the Super-Soldier Serum nonetheless inspires others to try to produce their own Super-Soldier.

1 Ba **Am** Captain America	7 Ba **Bw** Black Widow	17 St **Lc** Luke Cage	29 Vo **Se** Sentry	24 Re **Ta** Taskmaster	22 St **Uj** Union Jack	58 St **Ib** Isaiah Bradley
59 St **Jx** Justice	60 St **Sd** Soldier Supreme	18 Vo **Ms** Master Man	21 Vo **Ww** Warrior Woman	30 Vo **Ac** Anti-Cap	28 Vo **Dp** Deadpool	56 St **Fx** Fantomex
57 Vo **Hu** Huntsman	55 Vo **Sf** Stepford Cuckoos	51 To **Ti** Tarantula	39 St **Ra** Destroyer (Roger Aubrey)			

Tx TOXIC AGENT

While some chemical reactions have poisonous outcomes, not all result in individuals who are a plague on society.

34 St **Mr** Spider-Man (Miles Morales)

9 Vo **Gg** Green Goblin	26 Vo **Hb** Hobgoblin	33 Vo **Me** Menace	2 To **Re** Red Skull	12 To **Pu** Purple Man	27 To **Pw** Purple Woman	36 To **Pc** Purple Children

PYM PARTICLES

The amazing discovery of subatomic, size-changing particles is a giant leap forward for Super Heroes, although the breakthrough also proves helpful to villains.

3 Vo	5 Ba	23 St	32 St	38 Vo	13 St	37 St
An	**Ws**	**La**	**Cs**	**Ye**	**Go**	**Wn**
Ant-Man (Hank Pym)	The Wasp (Janet Van Dyne)	Ant-Man (Scott Lang)	Stinger	Yellowjacket	Goliath	The Wasp (Nadia Van Dyne)

ENERGY CONVERSION

Many individuals, whether by accident or design, learn how to harness energies from Earth and beyond to empower themselves.

11 Vo	25 St	19 Co	8 Co	20 Vo	54 Vo	52 Vo
Wo	**Rb**	**Ja**	**Ec**	**Wi**	**As**	**Nf**
Wonder Man	Spectrum	Jack of Hearts	Electro	Will O' The Wisp	Atlas (Erik Josten)	Nefarius

47 Vo	45 Vo
Ct	**Un**
Count Nefaria	Unicorn

UNSTABLE FORMULAS

Some people succeed in discovering what scholars have sought for centuries—the secret to a long life or even immortality, or just a cure for disease or injury.

4 Ba	35 St	31 St	15 St	42 St	43 St	49 St
Fy	**Fu**	**Bb**	**Mc**	**Vs**	**Ze**	**Zm**
Nick Fury	Nick Fury Jr.	Winter Soldier	Mockingbird	Baron von Strucker	Baron Heinrich Zemo	Baron Helmut Zemo

46 St	50 St	10 Vo	6 Vo	14 To	16 St	41 Vo
Di	**Cg**	**Kh**	**Lz**	**Mt**	**Mo**	**Hd**
Diablo	Cagliostro	Kraven the Hunter	Lizard	Man-Thing	Morbius	Mister Hyde

53 St	40 Re	48 St	44 St
Jf	**Ch**	**Nh**	**Gy**
Jack Flag	Chameleon	Nighthawk	Grey Gargoyle

CAPTAIN AMERICA

REAL NAME: Steve Rogers **POWERS:** Super-strength, speed, durability, stamina, agility, and reflexes; slowed aging **FIRST APPEARANCE:** *Captain America Comics* #1 (Mar 1941)

There is nobody who personifies the scientific miracles that occur in chemical reactions more than Captain America. Steve Rogers is a young man deemed so sickly and weak that he is not able to enlist in the army—he is instead selected to be the test subject of a top-secret program named Project: Rebirth. The brainchild of scientist Dr. Abraham Erskine, Rebirth is intended to create an army of Super-Soldiers, their physiology enhanced using a mixture of chemicals and radiation. Rogers is injected with the Super-Soldier Serum and then put into a metal chamber to be blasted with Vita-Rays—radiation intended to both speed up the effects of the serum and stabilize Rogers's body as it assimilates it.

The experiment is a total success—the Rogers who emerges from the chamber is a perfect human, whose every attribute has been boosted to peak conceivable levels. He is taller, broader, and more muscular; he can move as fast as the greatest-ever athlete; and his reflexes and agility are second to none. Tragically, Dr. Erskine is killed by a Nazi spy immediately after Rogers's transformation, and the exact composition of the Super-Soldier Serum is lost with him. Instead of being part of a new army of Super-Soldiers, Captain America is destined to be unique.

MAN OF WAR

Captain America, aka Cap, uses his new abilities to do what he wanted to do all along—join the war effort. In the last days of World War II, he is apparently lost at sea while preventing an unmanned plane from completing a bomb

attack. However,
another miracle
of science saves
him, and Cap
is preserved,
unharmed, in
the Arctic ice
before being
discovered
decades later
by the Avengers,
whose ranks
he soon joins.
Cap's unmatched
tactical and strategic
instincts are as much
of an asset to the team
as his enhanced abilities.
As well as his physical
attributes, Cap is aided in his fight for justice
by his famous shield. Made of a unique
Vibranium and Proto-Adamantium steel alloy,
it is light but incredibly strong. When Captain
America uses it as a throwing weapon in a fight,
he can throw it in such a way that its momentum
and kinetic energy will guide it back to him like
a boomerang. Like the Super-Soldier Serum,
the exact makeup of Cap's shield is unknown,
so it is impossible to reproduce it.
Captain America is a man out of time and
a unique human being. While chemistry has
granted him the physical advantages that enable
him to line up alongside superhumans and godlike
beings, it is his good heart and his innate sense
of right and wrong that make far more powerful
individuals respect him as a leader.

BLACK WIDOW

REAL NAME: Natasha Romanoff **POWERS:** Super-strength, speed, durability, stamina, agility, and reflexes; slowed aging **FIRST APPEARANCE:** *Tales of Suspense* #52 (Jan 1964)

While scientists in the West were trying to perfect the Super-Soldier Serum, their Soviet counterparts were working on their own version. This was deployed as part of the Black Widow Ops Program, an intense training initiative for female spies. Not only were the Black Widows given a thorough education in classic tools of espionage and top-level combat training, they were also given a cocktail of chemicals to make them human weapons.

RED ROOM

One such Black Widow is Natasha Romanoff, an orphan groomed from an early age to serve her country. While still a child at the school for spies known as the Red Room, Romanoff is given a psychochemical serum that implants false memories of being trained as a ballerina in her mind and actually induces an extreme pain reaction if she tries to think about her past too deeply. After her mind is made a supposedly malleable tool of the state, Romanoff goes on to complete her training at Department X, a super-

science facility creating enhanced agents for the motherland. Here, she is again injected with chemical serums to push her body to the peak of its capacity. As well as developing enhanced physical abilities, Romanoff's aging process is also dramatically slowed.

Despite graduating as an elite Black Widow—one of the best agents the Soviet Union has ever produced—Romanoff does not serve her Soviet masters for long. Although the mental conditioning is something she struggles with for the rest of her life, as is the guilt from the terrible deeds she committed for her country, she is able to shake off her programming and defect to the West. She then puts her augmented abilities to work fighting against injustice wherever she finds it.

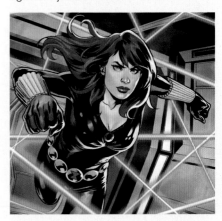

In addition to her Red Room enhancements, Black Widow also wears gauntlets that contain gadgets, including a Widow's Bite electric shock function.

LUKE CAGE

REAL NAME: Carl Lucas **POWERS:** Super-strength and stamina; invulnerability; healing factor
FIRST APPEARANCE: *Hero for Hire* #1 (Mar 1972)

While incarcerated for a crime he did not commit, Luke Cage (then known as Carl Lucas) reluctantly volunteers to be a guinea pig for an experimental serum, hoping that his helpfulness will increase his chances of parole. The serum has been devised by Dr. Noah Burstein and is based on the Super-Soldier Serum used to create Captain America. The serum's scientific foundation is cell regeneration, which, if accelerated, could make the human body recover more quickly from illness and injury and decelerate the aging process. Dr. Burstein is eager to test out his serum on Cage because he is already a strong and healthy subject—he stands the best chance of coming through the process with no ill effects.

POWER MAN

The first stage of the experiment is to immerse Cage in a bath of chemicals, then run electricity around him to create an electrical field. However, a bitter and racist prison guard tampers with the process, causing the dose of electricity

Cage is given to be vastly increased with the intention of killing him. However, it has the opposite effect—Cage's strength and durability are enhanced to superhuman levels. The prison guards soon discover that Cage's skin is now bulletproof, and he is able to simply smash through the brick walls of the prison and escape. Cage then builds a new life for himself as a hero for hire. Later, he has a daughter with fellow Super Hero Jessica Jones.

While unbreakable skin is a useful attribute in the battles Cage fights, it also has its disadvantages. If he were ever to need medical treatment that requires an incision, regular hospital equipment would not be able to pierce his skin. He would have to turn to a doctor who has access to high-grade lasers or Adamantium.

Luke Cage's cells are super-dense, meaning that he can withstand almost any injury, even close-range gunfire. His skin is reportedly as strong as steel.

SENTRY

REAL NAME: Robert Reynolds **POWERS:** Almost limitless physical powers—equivalent to a million exploding suns; psionic powers; immortality **FIRST APPEARANCE:** *Sentry* #1 (Sep 2000)

Following World War II, a joint initiative is set up between Canada and the US to pool their knowledge of the Weapon X and Super-Soldier programs and come up with something many thousands of times more powerful than the original Super-Soldier Serum. Many years pass, and the scientific work on "Project: Sentry" becomes siloed and unregulated. A professor, outsourced and unaware of what he is really working on, comes up with a new version of the serum. One of his students, a schizophrenic drug addict named Robert Reynolds, steals the chemical solution and swallows it. He instantaneously becomes the most powerful human on the planet—and the most dangerous. While the Sentry only wants to do good, his evil other self, the Void, is an existential threat.

TASKMASTER

REAL NAME: Tony Masters **POWERS:** Photographic reflexes—duplicating any form of combat or other skills he sees **FIRST APPEARANCE:** *Avengers* #195 (May 1980)

Tony Masters is born with the ability to mimic any ability that he sees, in person or on screen. He later heightens his natural talent to superhuman levels when he injects himself with a corrupted version of the Super-Soldier Serum, designed to enhance the human brain's ability to absorb knowledge. Masters can instantly recall any knowledge committed to his so-called implicit memory, although he struggles to remember details from his explicit memory, which holds the actual people and events of his life. It seems that he has limited space in his brain for the new knowledge he acquires. While Taskmaster is ostensibly a villain, it is later revealed that he is a deep-cover S.H.I.E.L.D. agent whose secret is maintained because even he can't remember who he truly is.

UNION JACK

REAL NAME: Brian Falsworth **POWERS:** Enhanced strength, speed, durability, stamina, agility, and reflexes; electricity bolts **FIRST APPEARANCE:** *Invaders* #18 (Jul 1977)

When the famous German biochemist Eric Schmitt is imprisoned by the Nazis during World War II, his health begins to fail him. Close to death, he entrusts a vial of a formula he has been working on to his cellmate, British aristocrat Brian Falsworth, pleading with him to not let it fall into Nazi hands. Falsworth decides that the best way of ensuring that can never happen is to drink the unknown formula. He soon discovers that the formula is a version of the Super-Soldier Serum, which the Nazis have been trying to recreate ever since it was used to turn Steve Rogers into Captain America. Falsworth is immediately rendered stronger, faster, and more agile. He escapes the prison and becomes the costumed Super Hero Destroyer, fighting against the Nazis in their own backyard. Falsworth later adopts the costume and identity of Union Jack, which was previously worn by his father, Lord Montgomery Falsworth. After an encounter with the Asgardian god Thor and his hammer, Mjolnir, Falsworth also gains electrical powers, giving him the ability to discharge bolts of electricity from his body. When Falsworth later gives up the Union Jack identity, working-class hero Joey Chapman takes it on.

ANCILLARY EXEMPLARS

Isaiah Bradley is one of hundreds of African American soldiers forcibly recruited to take part in the US Army's attempt to recreate the Super-Soldier Serum. He is one of the few survivors of the experiments, and although he does gain abilities and uses them to serve his country, he also suffers severe mental side effects. Bradley's son, Josiah, is created in a lab, where he is genetically engineered to have all of his father's powers with none of the drawbacks. He later fights crime as **Justice**, armed with his father's shield. A more bizarre carrier of the Super-Soldier Serum is found in Warp World, a dimension created using the Soul Gem, where the Super-Soldier Serum has magical properties. Here, Captain America is merged with mystical Sorcerer Supreme Doctor Strange to make the **Soldier Supreme**.

MASTER MAN

REAL NAME: Wilhelm Lohmer **POWERS:** Super-strength, stamina, and durability; levitation **FIRST APPEARANCE:** *Giant-Size Invaders* #1 (Mar 1975)

During World War II, Wilhelm Lohmer, an American of German descent, is chosen by the Nazis to be their equivalent of Captain America. German spies in the US capture Dr. Murray Anderson, who works on Project: Rebirth, and use a device to extract information about the Super-Soldier Serum from Anderson's brain. They then infuse Lohmer with a serum based on the data they extract and give him the Nazi propaganda-friendly name Master Man. In addition to all of the superhuman attributes that are bestowed on Captain America in the original Project: Rebirth, Master Man can also deploy a form of psionic levitation, which allows him to fly through the air.

WARRIOR WOMAN

REAL NAME: Julia Koenig **POWERS:** Super-strength, speed, durability, stamina, and agility; tactical awareness **FIRST APPEARANCE:** *Invaders* #17 (Jun 1977)

Julia Koenig is a Nazi spy based in London during World War II. She captures and hypnotizes an American cartoonist who has links to Project: Rebirth and forces the hapless artist to reveal everything he knows about the Super-Soldier Serum. Koenig then decides to use that information to create a serum that she can use on herself to powerfully demonstrate to Adolf Hitler that women can do more for the Fatherland than rearing children and keeping house. When Koenig is caught in an explosion in her laboratory, she transforms into Warrior Woman, a "perfect" human specimen, albeit one devoted to the fascist cause.

ANTI-CAP

REAL NAME: Unknown **POWERS:** Super-strength; enhanced stamina; healing factor **FIRST APPEARANCE:** *Captain America and the Falcon* #1 (Mar 2004)

The true identity of the man who becomes Anti-Cap is unknown, but he is a US Navy SEAL, prohibited from active service due to psychological issues. He is chosen instead for an experimental process to create a Super-Soldier for the US Navy. A serum is administered based on that which empowers Luke Cage. As well as the initial dose, there is a spinal implant and patches for his skin that keep releasing doses into his body to stop the soldier's abilities from fading. It seems that the process has failed until the soldier experiences a near-death experience, the adrenaline from which triggers the effects of the serum. However, the serum also combines with the subject's existing mental issues to make him go rogue.

DEADPOOL

REAL NAME: Wade Wilson **POWERS:** Super-strength, speed, stamina, durability, reflexes, and agility; healing factor **FIRST APPEARANCE:** *New Mutants* #98 (Feb 1991)

When mercenary Wade Wilson is diagnosed with cancer, he agrees to undergo the Weapon X procedure in the hopes that the powers it will grant him will also stave off the disease. To achieve this outcome, Wilson is given genetic material from previous Weapon X subject Wolverine, gaining his phenomenal healing factor. The cancer is beaten, and Wilson is now practically invulnerable to any other disease or injury. Like Wolverine, the healing factor also enables Wilson to hugely boost his levels of strength, speed, stamina, and reflexes. He later adopts the name Deadpool after being experimented on by unscrupulous scientists who take bets on which of their unfortunate subjects will die first. Deadpool's many traumatic experiences have left him in a permanently unstable mental state.

ANCILLARY EXEMPLARS

Weapon Plus is one of the many organizations trying to recreate the Super-Soldier Serum. Eventually, its scientists specialize in creating living weapons designed for mutant-hunting. One of the outcomes of their experiments is **Fantomex**—the result of splicing Sentinel technology with chemicals to create a super-techno-organic hybrid. Also created by Weapon Plus is **Huntsman**, who is intended to be a Super-Sentinel and has a dangerous hive-mind ability. Next on the production line are the psionic **Stepford Cuckoos**, identical mutant girls genetically engineered from eggs taken from the powerful mutant telepath Emma Frost. Away from Weapon Plus, the **Tarantula** is injected with a chemical serum to become a twisted version of Captain America for the South American dictatorship of Delvadia. And Roger Aubrey is given a derivative of the Super-Soldier Serum, taking on the heroic identity of the **Destroyer**.

SPIDER-MAN
(MILES MORALES)

34   St
Mr
Spider-Man
(Miles Morales)

REAL NAME: Miles Morales **POWERS:** Super-strength, speed, durability, and balance; wall-crawling; venom blasts; camouflage; healing factor **FIRST APPEARANCE:** *Ultimate Fallout* #4 (Oct 2011)

Like the Spider-Man of Earth-616, Earth-1610's Miles Morales obtains amazing powers from a spider bite. Unlike the original, this spider is not radioactive but, instead, genetically altered—infused with the so-called Oz Formula. This concoction is created by that reality's Norman Osborn, drawing on the blood of Nick Fury and Steve Rogers in the hopes of coming up with a new and improved Super-Soldier Serum. The formula is injected into test animals, including spiders, to monitor its effects. One of these spiders escapes from Osborn's Oscorp in the bag of a thief, Aaron Davis. Later, the arachnid bites Davis's young nephew, Miles Morales, transferring the Oz Formula to him, as well as the spider's own DNA.

ULTIMATE POWER

The method of transmission means that Morales is not quite like other spider-powered beings. The spider's venom contains an element of Super-Soldier Serum, but he is not exactly like other Super-Soldiers either. The toxic agents of the venom combine with the Oz Formula and result in something quite different. After coming around from the shock of the bite, the first power Morales discovers he has is a form of camouflage so effective that it resembles invisibility, something not shared by either Super-Soldiers or Spider-Totems. The second unusual ability manifests a short time later, when Morales inadvertently fends off a bully by giving him an electric shock with his hands.

A further major difference between Morales and his reality's Peter Parker is that Morales immediately confides

in someone about his powers—his best friend, Ganke Lee. Even though Morales believes himself to be a mutant, it is Ganke who makes the connection between his friend's powers coming from a spider bite and the hero Spider-Man. Testing Ganke's theory, Morales discovers that |it is true and that he can crawl on vertical and horizontal surfaces. He also seems to have an extremely sensitive spider-sense, which warns him of danger to an even greater degree than the original Spider-Man's.

When Earth-1610's Peter Parker is killed saving his family from Electro, Morales steps up to take on the mantle of Spider-Man. He is later bequeathed Parker's old web-shooters, giving him yet another of Spider-Man's classic abilities. Morales is saved from the destruction of Earth-1610 during the incursions when he is transported to the patchwork planet Battleworld.

After the restoration of the Multiverse, his reality is not brought back, so Morales makes a new life on Earth-616 instead. As a reward for his kindness toward Molecule Man, Morales's parents and friends are also recreated to live on Earth-616, just as if they had always been there. This gives the young hero a chance to learn how to be a hero from Peter Parker, something that fate had denied him in his home reality.

GREEN GOBLIN

REAL NAME: Norman Osborn **POWERS:** Super-strength, speed, stamina, and agility; healing factor; genius intelligence **FIRST APPEARANCE:** *Amazing Spider-Man* #14 (Jul 1964)

Chemical reactions do not come much more volatile than the one that turns unscrupulous businessman Norman Osborn into the Green Goblin. Nothing is more important to Osborn than the wielding of power, and he will stop at nothing in his pursuit of it. He frames his business partner so that he can assume total control of their company, Oscorp. Then he takes his partner's idea for a formula that will give increased strength and intelligence and creates it, intending to use it on himself. However, Osborn's plan literally and figuratively blows up in his face. Following the explosion, he is indeed stronger and smarter but also seriously mentally unstable. He embarks on a criminal career as the Green Goblin, terrorizing New York City and making a particular enemy out of Spider-Man.

FAMILY BUSINESS

Norman and his only son, Harry, have a difficult and distant relationship, exacerbated by the death of Harry's mother and Norman's obsession with work. Norman has little time for his son, and Harry feels rejected and ignored by his father. After Harry witnesses his father's apparent demise during a fierce battle with Spider-Man, Harry exposes himself to the Goblin Formula and takes up the mantle of the Green Goblin. At first, he exhibits the same powers as his father, but Harry later discovers that Norman had been tinkering with the formula to make himself stronger. Following up on this theory, Harry makes another revised formula based on his father's work and gains even greater powers. However, like his father, it also comes at the cost of his sanity.

The Green Goblin uses his talent for invention to come up with a range of signature weapons, including Pumpkin Bombs and the Goblin Glider.

HOBGOBLIN

REAL NAME: Roderick Kingsley **POWERS:** Super-strength, speed, stamina, durability, and agility; healing factor; genius intellect **FIRST APPEARANCE:** *Amazing Spider-Man* #238 (Mar 1983)

Like Norman Osborn, Roderick Kingsley initially uses the Goblin Formula to increase his own clout in the business world. Kingsley is a fashion designer who happens upon an old hideout of Osborn's, discovering a cache of equipment, costumes, and the deadly formula there. Kingsley is a cunning operator, possibly even more so than Osborn. He creates confusion and mystery around his Hobgoblin persona by sometimes coercing others to take on the identity in his place. He also uses his intellect to tweak the original formula to minimize the psychological side effects and exposes himself to the chemicals in a more limited way. In spite of that, Hobgoblin's enhanced strength after taking the formula is comparable to the Green Goblin's.

MENACE

REAL NAME: Lily Hollister **POWERS:** Super-strength, speed, stamina, durability, agility, and reflexes **FIRST APPEARANCE:** *Amazing Spider-Man* #549 (Mar 2008)

Lily Hollister does not expose herself to the Goblin Formula in a bid for greater power. As Harry Osborn's girlfriend, she unintentionally stumbles upon a stash of equipment belonging to Harry's father, spilling some vials of the formula. When it gets onto her skin and is rapidly absorbed, it becomes clear that Norman Osborn had been tinkering again with the makeup of the formula. Not only does Hollister gain superhuman abilities, but her physical form also grows and mutates to take on a gray, goblinlike appearance. She makes the most of her new abilities by running a terror campaign to boost her own father's mayoral election hopes. Later, she is depowered using a serum formulated by Parker Industries from the blood of her friend Carlie Cooper, who had been transformed into the goblinlike Monster.

RED SKULL

REAL NAME: Johann Shmidt **POWERS:** Transference of consciousness to new bodies; genius intellect **FIRST APPEARANCE:** *Captain America Comics* #7 (Oct 1941)

Johann Shmidt is not born with super-powers—merely all-encompassing hate and an advanced intellect. He uses that intellect to plot his rise in the world, first within the Third Reich, centered on his native Germany, then expanding his ambitions even beyond that. He is Hitler's right-hand man for a time, wearing a Red Skull mask to terrorize enemies of the regime. However, Shmidt does not like playing second fiddle to anyone, even the Führer, and starts making plans of his own.

The Red Skull's weapon of choice is created in a laboratory from a lethal concoction of chemicals. The "Dust of Death" is a toxin that causes the skin on a victim's head to turn red, shrivel, and then tighten and all their hair to fall out. Death follows rapidly, and the corpse's face is frozen in a permanent rictus grin.

BACK TO LIFE

Poison is not the Red Skull's only weapon—he has also achieved a kind of immortality, as he has the technology to transfer his consciousness into other bodies. This incredible scientific advance is first achieved by fellow Nazi Dr. Arnim Zola, who uses his knowledge of the process to bring Red Skull back to life in a cloned body of Steve Rogers (Captain America). After this rebirth, the Red Skull gains enhanced powers of his own, as if he himself has taken the Super-Soldier Serum. Later, the perfection of this new body is tarnished when Shmidt accidentally inhales his own Dust of Death. The enhanced durability of the cloned body stops him from dying but his face is permanently disfigured into the Red Skull form.

His obsessive, decades-long hatred for Captain America means that Red Skull's plans almost always revolve around trying to destroy his archnemesis.

PURPLE MAN

REAL NAME: Zebediah Killgrave **POWERS:** Mind control using pheromones; healing factor **FIRST APPEARANCE:** *Daredevil* #4 (Oct 1964)

Zebediah Killgrave is a foreign spy who breaks into a US military facility to steal a sample of an experimental nerve gas. The mission goes wrong, and Killgrave is accidentally doused in the gas. The chemicals fuse with acids in his own body to turn his skin purple, but there is another, far more powerful, change in him. He now has the superhuman ability to exert a persuasive mental influence over anyone near him by secreting pheromones, with the exception of individuals who have unusually strong willpower, like Daredevil. The Man Without Fear also correctly surmises that Purple Man's chemically induced powers over others can be stopped with a barrier, like specially treated plastic sheeting.

PURPLE WOMAN

REAL NAME: Kara Killgrave **POWERS:** Mind control using pheromones **FIRST APPEARANCE:** *Alpha Flight* #41 (Dec 1986)

The Purple Man's daughter, Kara Killgrave, inherits his chemically altered DNA, although her abilities do not manifest until she reaches puberty.

Her skin suddenly turns purple, and she is able to secrete pheromones that enable her to control the behavior of anyone near her. Unlike her father, the subjects of her mind control also turn purple until they are freed from her influence. At first, Kara is terrified of the ramifications of what she can do, so she seeks help from the superteam Alpha Flight. Here, she finds camaraderie among others who know what it is to carry the burden of power and decides to use her abilities for good.

PURPLE CHILDREN

POWERS: Mind control using pheromones; empathetic powers **FIRST APPEARANCE:** *Daredevil* #8 (Sep 2014)

The Purple Children are the offspring of Zebediah Killgrave, who uses his mind-control powers to make women fall in love with him and then impregnates them. After many years, Killgrave gathers all his children and activates their mind-control powers, hoping to find unconditional love for the first time. However, he soon discovers that his children have an advantage over him—they can unite their powers to control him. They force their father to step in front of a moving train, then strike out on their own. The Purple Children retain their powers as long as they are all near each other. When their father returns, the children stay together as a team to keep watch on him and try to curb his evil activities.

ANT-MAN (HANK PYM)

REAL NAME: Hank Pym **POWERS:** Changing size using Pym Particles; genius intellect; communication with insects **FIRST APPEARANCE:** *Tales to Astonish* #27 (Jan 1962)

Brilliant scientist Dr. Hank Pym discovers a new type of subatomic particle. Pym's research reveals that these "Pym Particles," if converted into a serum, can shrink objects and organisms to a tiny size. Another version of the serum brings a shrunken item back to its proper size. After trying the formula on himself and almost getting killed in an anthill, Pym pours the serums away, but he later mixes a new batch. He also studies the behavior of ants and builds himself a helmet that "tunes in" to the frequency of the ants' electrical impulses. Wearing this cybernetic helmet, Pym can communicate with ants and even command them. As Ant-Man, Pym is only half an inch (1.27 centimeters) high, but he retains the strength of a full-grown human. He also designs a costume that can shrink and grow with his body.

SMALL WORLDS

Using the Pym Particles is more than just a matter of changing size. When Pym, or any other user, shrinks, the mass lost from the body is shifted to another dimension. Later, when Pym finds a way to grow to giant size, Pym's serum causes his body to "borrow" mass from another dimension. He can also shrink to subatomic size and enter an alternate dimension known as the Microverse. Eventually, Pym's cumulative exposure to the Pym Particles is so great that his body can replicate their effects without the need for a serum. However, the strain of using them begins to take its toll on him. Pym's erratic and sometimes violent behavior leads to the breakup of his marriage and, ultimately, to his retirement from Super Heroics.

When Hank Pym uses Pym Particles to grow to a huge size, he adopts the identity of Giant-Man. His other code names include Goliath and Yellowjacket.

THE WASP (JANET VAN DYNE)

REAL NAME: Janet Van Dyne **POWERS:** Changing size using Pym Particles; flight; bioelectrical blasts; communication with insects **FIRST APPEARANCE:** *Tales to Astonish* #44 (Jun 1963)

By the time Janet Van Dyne meets Hank Pym (Ant-Man), his research into Pym Particles has progressed from ants to wasps, and he can now trigger mutations in a human that will give them wings and antennae. Van Dyne's scientist father has recently been killed, and she is determined to avenge his death, so she agrees to undergo Pym's procedure. He implants synthetic cells under her skin to enable her to shrink to a tiny size and grow wings and antennae, although at normal size her wasp features will disappear. The antennae Van Dyne grows work like Pym's cybernetic helmet, enabling her to communicate with insects. Pym also designs a costume made from unstable molecules that will shrink and grow as The Wasp transforms. Her transformations are triggered using a gas made from Pym Particles, rather than the serum Pym uses in his early days.

THE STING

Later, Pym invents a wrist-mounted weapon for Van Dyne to wear: her wasp's sting. At first, it is a compressed air gun, but it is later upgraded to harness bioelectricity from her body and fire it out in blasts. Her long exposure to Pym Particles eventually enables Van Dyne to manifest her stings and all her other abilities organically, without the use of external stimuli.

Van Dyne goes on to show that she is so much more than a mere sidekick to Hank Pym. Her natural leadership qualities and inherent positivity shine out when she is called upon to chair the Avengers, of which she is a founding member.

As well as flight and size reduction, The Wasp is able to grow to a large size, but this power causes her extreme exertion, so she uses it as a last resort.

ANT-MAN (SCOTT LANG)

REAL NAME: Scott Lang **POWERS:** Changing size using Pym Particles; communication with insects; increased strength and durability **FIRST APPEARANCE:** *Marvel Premiere* #47 (Apr 1979)

Scott Lang is a former criminal trying to go straight when he discovers that his beloved daughter, Cassie, is dying of a heart condition. Desperate to get Cassie a lifesaving operation, Lang robs the home of Dr. Hank Pym, stealing his Ant-Man suit and cybernetic helmet. The suit's belt contains gas canisters that enable Lang to shrink, while the helmet allows him to summon and command ants with his mind. He uses the equipment to sneak into Cross Industries, where there is a doctor who can help Cassie. Unbeknownst to Lang, the suit's former owner, Hank Pym, observes Lang in action and, afterward, gives the suit and helmet—and his blessing—to Lang, who becomes the new Ant-Man.

MORE THAN MEETS THE EYE

Lang may not appear to be on the same intellectual plane as Pym, but he is in fact the first person to discover how the Pym Particles he uses as Ant-Man really work. The fact that his strength and durability are so great at giant size, and remain at

normal levels at ant size, does not seem to add up. Lang studies the history of the Pym Particles and extrapolates that they operate not only on the axis of size, but also on two other axes—of strength and durability. Using this knowledge, Lang devises a way to increase his strength and durability enough to give Latverian Super Villain Doctor Doom a severe drubbing, although the effort puts his body under great strain.

Scott Lang has been a convict, an engineer, a security expert, and an Avenger, but his most important role is always being a good father to his daughter.

Using flying ants for transportation is just one benefit of Scott Lang's connection with insects. He can also use bees in the same way.

STINGER

REAL NAME: Cassie Lang **POWERS:** Changing size using Pym Particles **FIRST APPEARANCE:** *New Avengers* #6 (Sep 2005)

Cassie Lang wants to be just like her dad, Scott, aka Ant-Man, so she steals Pym Particles from him. Repeated exposure to them over the years gives her organic size-changing powers. She joins the Young Avengers superteam as Stature but is killed by Doctor Doom. The villain later uses magic to resurrect Lang, who returns without her powers. She tries to live a normal life but is drawn back into being a Super Hero when the Power Broker Process gives her the chance to regain her abilities.

YELLOWJACKET

REAL NAME: Darren Cross **POWERS:** Changing size using Pym Particles; enhanced strength and senses; healing factor **FIRST APPEARANCE:** *Astonishing Ant-Man* #12 (Nov 2016)

Ruthless businessman Darren Cross accesses Pym Particles by stealing Cassie Lang's heart, which is infused with them. Empowered, he becomes the villain Yellowjacket, appropriating a former identity of Hank Pym's. Cross differs from other Pym Particle users in that his size changes are triggered by his emotions. Cross also has enhanced strength and senses, plus an accelerated healing factor, from a device he invents: a Nucleorganic Pacemaker.

GOLIATH

REAL NAME: Clint Barton **POWERS:** Changing size using Pym Particles **FIRST APPEARANCE:** *Avengers* #63 (Apr 1969)

When Hank Pym finds a way to grow to giant size, he takes on the identity of Goliath, but he comes to associate the name with troubled times. He packs away his costume and growth serum, but they are retrieved by Clint Barton, aka Hawkeye, who is desperate for a size advantage in a mission. Barton does not use Pym Particles, or the Goliath identity, long enough to give him permanent size-changing powers.

THE WASP (NADIA VAN DYNE)

REAL NAME: Nadia Van Dyne **POWERS:** Changing size; flight; bioelectrical blasts **FIRST APPEARANCE:** Free Comic Book Day, *Civil War II*, 1 (May 2016)

Nadia is the secret daughter of Hank Pym. She is brought up in the Red Room, where she trains to be a spy, but she is encouraged to pursue scientific discovery like her father. Nadia teaches herself to use Pym Particles and escapes the Red Room, traveling to the US. Here, she learns Hank Pym is dead, but she forms a bond with Janet Van Dyne. She eventually takes on her Wasp identity and her last name.

WONDER MAN

REAL NAME: Simon Williams **POWERS:** Super-strength; invulnerability; enhanced senses; flight; immortality; energy manipulation **FIRST APPEARANCE:** *Avengers* #9 (Oct 1964)

Simon Williams is a businessman who has fallen on hard times when he is persuaded to undergo a process devised by terrorist mastermind Baron Zemo in his South American laboratory. Williams is bathed in an intense concentration of ionic rays to increase his strength and durability and make him a living engine of destruction. However, the new Wonder Man learns that the rays that give him his power have also changed his metabolism and will kill him within a week unless a regular antidote is supplied by Zemo. Williams later decides to use his powers for good and accepts that he will die. However, he merely falls into a deathlike coma and is later revived with a more energized form and even greater powers.

SPECTRUM

REAL NAME: Monica Rambeau **POWERS:** Energy absorption and conversion; flight; speed; intangibility; invisibility **FIRST APPEARANCE:** *Amazing Spider-Man Annual* #16 (Oct 1982)

Harbor patrol officer Monica Rambeau is investigating a mysterious weapon that draws energy from other dimensions when she is caught in an explosion.

After she comes around, she realizes that she can change her body into any form of energy, including gamma, infrared, and electricity. This involves her summoning the required energy from another dimension and replacing it there with her regular body cells. First fighting as the new Captain Marvel, Rambeau also takes the identities of Photon and Pulsar. Spectrum's powers are later enhanced when fellow Mighty Avenger Blue Marvel infuses her body with extra photons.

JACK OF HEARTS

REAL NAME: Jonathan Hart **POWERS:** Super-strength, speed, stamina, and durability; flight; healing factor **FIRST APPEARANCE:** *Deadly Hands of Kung Fu* #22 (Mar 1976)

With a mother who is an alien Contraxian, Jack Hart is already different from most people. He becomes even more unique when he is doused in Zero Fluid—a new type of fuel invented by his father. Hart's cells mutate, and he now has the ability to emit huge blasts of energy. He also gains super-strength and other powers that are so great that Hart has trouble controlling them. So he is forced to wear a special armored suit to help him do so. Eventually, the Avengers provide Hart with a neutro-mist to dampen his powers so that he can take his armor off safely. Hart later dies in space but is reanimated by an insane Scarlet Witch during an attack on Avengers Mansion, which results in his powers causing a devastating explosion.

ELECTRO

REAL NAME: Max Dillon **POWERS:** Creating and harnessing electrical energy; energy blasts; wall-crawling **FIRST APPEARANCE:** *Amazing Spider-Man* #9 (Feb 1964)

Money-obsessed power-line worker Max Dillon is working alone at the top of a utility pole, holding electrical cables, when lightning strikes. Due to the way he is holding the wires, Dillon is not killed, but the massive jolt of electricity transforms him. His body has become a living generator—he can fire out electrical blasts from his hands or charge his skin so that anyone who touches him gets a massive electric shock. The constant production of electricity within his body is powered by minuscule contractions in his muscles. Dillon later rigs up an electricity lab with a machine that can charge him still further, increasing his power.

WILL O' THE WISP

REAL NAME: Jackson Arvad **POWERS:** Super-strength and density; flight; intangibility **FIRST APPEARANCE:** *Amazing Spider-Man* #167 (Apr 1977)

Jackson Arvad is a scientist working in electromagnetic research who is driven to ever greater efforts by an uncaring boss. One day, Arvad is caught in a gravimetric power surge, shattering the magno-chamber he is working with. The accident destabilizes the magnetic connection between the molecules of his body, making them disperse, and his boss leaves him to die. However, instead of dying, Arvad is transformed into a hugely energized being who can become either intangible or super-dense. He can fly and harness energy to fire super-charged blasts. He can even use the light created as a by-product of his power to hypnotize people.

ANCILLARY EXEMPLARS

Like Wonder Man, Erik Josten is empowered by ionic energy, but he also later uses Pym Particles to become the giant **Atlas**. Another individual with ionic powers is **Nefarius**, although he has previously also used energy from a mystic moonstone. He models his villainous look on **Count Nefaria**, who assembles a team of ionically powered beings and also gains these powers himself. Meanwhile, the **Unicorn** has the unique ability to harness a variety of different energies and fire them in beams from his forehead.

NICK FURY

REAL NAME: Nicholas Fury **POWERS:** Peak human strength, speed, stamina, durability, agility, and reflexes; slowed aging **FIRST APPEARANCE:** *Sgt. Fury and His Howling Commandos* #1 (May 1963)

Nick Fury has been "The Man on the Wall," fighting off threats to Earth, since World War II. He has been able to do this because of a serum called the Infinity Formula, which has dramatically slowed down his aging process. The formula is created by a scientist named Professor Berthold Sternburg and is given to Fury after he sustains a life-threatening injury in France during the war. Said to be derived from the Elixir of Life, the Infinity Formula is not a one-time transformation—booster doses must be taken every year, although eventually Fury gains a cumulative effect from the serum and does not need to keep taking it. Fury is a key member of S.H.I.E.L.D. and is its director for many years, bringing his military experience to bear as a dedicated agent, leading from the front.

NICK FURY JR.

REAL NAME: Nicholas Fury Jr. **POWERS:** Peak human strength, speed, stamina, durability, agility, and reflexes; slowed aging **FIRST APPEARANCE:** *Battle Scars* #1 (Jan 2012)

Nick Fury Jr. has no need to take the Infinity Formula to prevent his body from aging because he is born with it in his blood—inherited from his father of the same name. He is also able to enhance his natural abilities further by using a specially designed battle suit, which has different modes depending on whether stealth or all-out action is required in any given mission situation. The suit can inject adrenalin and beta blockers directly into Fury Jr.'s bloodstream to temporarily increase his strength, speed, and precision. Fury follows his father in becoming an agent of S.H.I.E.L.D., and, sadly, he also follows his father in losing his left eye and wearing an eyepatch. While the elder Fury loses his eye to a Nazi grenade, Fury Jr.'s eye is cut out by the Leviathan terrorist organization.

WINTER SOLDIER

31	St
Bb	
Winter Soldier	

REAL NAME: James "Bucky" Barnes **POWERS:** Peak human strength, speed, and stamina; slowed aging; energy bolts
FIRST APPEARANCE: *Captain America* #1 (Jan 2005)

Presumed killed during WW II, Captain America's partner, "Bucky" Barnes, is actually captured by the Soviets. They give him a bionic arm to replace the one he loses in the war and brainwash him to become a ruthless assassin. Due to his apparent instability, Barnes is placed into cryostasis between missions to prevent aging. He eventually breaks free and returns to the US, where he uses his talents for good as the Winter Soldier. After being wounded on a mission, Nick Fury saves Barnes's life with the Infinity Formula, slowing his aging process once again.

MOCKINGBIRD

15	St
Mc	
Mockingbird	

REAL NAME: Barbara "Bobbi" Morse **POWERS:** Does not age; enhanced strength and agility; healing factor
FIRST APPEARANCE: *Astonishing Tales* #6 (Jun 1971)

"Bobbi" Morse is one of S.H.I.E.L.D.'s best agents and a regular Avenger when she is mortally wounded in the line of duty. Nick Fury saves her life by injecting her with a concoction first created by the Nazis during World War II, which combines their versions of the Super-Soldier Serum and the Infinity Formula. This substance not only awakens Morse from her coma and cures her gunshot wound, but it also seemingly stops her aging process and gives her enhanced strength and agility. However, as Fury warns, the cost could be that Mockingbird lives to bury all her friends.

ANCILLARY EXEMPLARS

42	St
Vs	
Baron von Strucker	

43	St
Ze	
Baron Heinrich Zemo	

49	St
Zm	
Baron Helmut Zemo	

46	St
Di	
Diablo	

50	St
Cg	
Cagliostro	

Many other individuals use exotic substances to curtail aging. **Baron von Strucker** contracts the Deathspore Virus and gains enhanced abilities and longevity. **Baron Heinrich Zemo**, whose Adhesive X causes his mask to be stuck to his face, also develops Compound X, which slows his aging process. His son, **Baron Helmut Zemo**, uses the same formula to retain his own youth. The alchemist **Diablo** discovers a potion for eternal youth and lives for 1,000 years. And the sorcerous **Cagliostro** creates a potion for immortality from a forbidden book.

KRAVEN THE HUNTER

REAL NAME: Sergei Kravinoff **POWERS:** Super-strength, speed, stamina, durability, agility, and reflexes; longevity; enhanced senses **FIRST APPEARANCE:** *Amazing Spider-Man* #15 (Aug 1964)

10	Vo

Kh

Kraven the Hunter

Sergei Kravinoff may be the ultimate hunter, but it is not just natural skill that has honed his predatory talents. He also enhances his strength, speed, stamina, and other attributes with a mysterious concoction known as the Calypso Serum.

Stolen from an African witch doctor, the potion slows down Kravinoff's aging process as well. However, the serum is found to induce rages and irrational behavior. Kravinoff takes a wider interest in chemicals and their applications and how they can affect others as well as himself. He uses a range of toxins and potions as part of his hunting arsenal. The mental instability caused by Kravinoff's use of the Calypso Serum seems to be eradicated after he dies and is brought back to life, and he begins to exhibit interests in things other than killing.

LIZARD

REAL NAME: Curt Connors **POWERS:** Super-strength; healing factor; wall-crawling; lizard features; communication with reptiles **FIRST APPEARANCE:** *Amazing Spider-Man* #6 (Nov 1963)

6	Vo

Lz

Lizard

Curt Connors is a big talent in multiple scientific fields, including biology, biochemistry, and medicine. When he loses an arm working as a military surgeon, Connors decides to formulate a serum to regrow missing limbs. Using

DNA from reptiles that regenerate limbs naturally, Connors comes up with a formula and uses it on himself. At first, the results are exactly what he wants— his arm grows back—but then there are side effects. Connors mutates into a vicious reptilian beast. After Spider-Man helps him find a cure to his "Lizard" condition, Connors, undeterred, gets back to trying to perfect his serum. But he again becomes the Lizard and seems cursed to wage an endless battle between his humane scientist self and his reptilian other half.

MAN-THING

14 To
Mt
Man-Thing

REAL NAME: Ted Sallis **POWERS:** Changing size and shape; regeneration; interdimensional travel; control of plant life **FIRST APPEARANCE:** *Savage Tales* #1 (May 1971)

US military biochemist Dr. Ted Sallis develops Serum SO-2, which protects individuals from toxins but also has one major drawback—it turns humans into monstrous beasts. When S.H.I.E.L.D. wants to use the formula as the basis for a new Super-Soldier Serum, Sallis moves to the Florida Everglades to work on it, but disaster strikes. After injecting himself with his serum to keep it from falling into the hands of evil organization A.I.M., Sallis crashes his car into the swamp. The serum reacts with the swamp to transform the scientist into the plant-beast Man-Thing.

MORBIUS

16 St
Mo
Morbius

REAL NAME: Michael Morbius **POWERS:** Super-strength and senses; healing factor; gliding; hypnotism **FIRST APPEARANCE:** *Amazing Spider-Man* #101 (Oct 1971)

Nobel Prize-winning scientist Dr. Michael Morbius must devote his genius to something very personal—trying to find a cure for his terminal blood disease. He creates a serum distilled from the blood of vampire bats, then takes a dose of it and gives himself an electric-shock treatment. Morbius becomes a living vampire and, horrified, tries to end his life in the ocean. However, his survival instinct kicks in and he surfaces, planning to feed on the blood of "lesser" mortals. Morbius's bite, like a vampire of legend, can turn other individuals into creatures like himself.

ANCILLARY EXEMPLARS

41 Vo
Hd
Mister Hyde

53 St
Jf
Jack Flag

40 Re
Ch
Chameleon

48 St
Nh
Nighthawk

44 St
Gy
Grey Gargoyle

There is no shortage of chemical concoctions that can have dramatic effects. The Hyde Formula turns Dr. Calvin Zabo into **Mister Hyde**, a massive, muscle-bound creature. **Jack Flag** is also saturated with the Hyde Formula and becomes super-strong.

The **Chameleon** takes a formula that renders his body malleable, taking his flair for disguise to new heights. **Nighthawk** creates the serum that gives him super-powers. And the **Grey Gargoyle** spills a contaminated solution that transforms his body and other objects to stone.

37
 38
 39
 40
 41
42

 43

 44
 45
46

47
48

 49
 50
 51
52
53

54
 55

56

57
58
 59
 60

1	Captain America	16	Stepford Cuckoos	28	The Wasp	39	Atlas	52	Kraven the Hunter
2	Black Widow	17	Tarantula		(Janet Van Dyne)		(Erik Josten)	53	Lizard
3	Luke Cage	18	Destroyer	29	Ant-Man	40	Nefarius	54	Man-Thing
4	Sentry	19	Spider-Man		(Scott Lang)	41	Count Nefaria	55	Morbius
5	Taskmaster		(Miles Morales)	30	Stinger	42	Unicorn	56	Mister Hyde
6	Union Jack	20	Green Goblin	31	Yellowjacket	43	Nick Fury	57	Jack Flag
7	Isaiah Bradley	21	Hobgoblin	32	Goliath	44	Nick Fury Jr.	58	Chameleon
8	Justice	22	Menace	33	The Wasp	45	Winter Soldier	59	Nighthawk
9	Soldier Supreme	23	Red Skull		(Nadia Van Dyne)	46	Mockingbird	60	Grey Gargoyle
10	Master Man	24	Purple Man	34	Wonder Man	47	Baron von Strucker		
11	Warrior Woman	25	Purple Woman	35	Spectrum	48	Baron Heinrich Zemo		
12	Anti-Cap	26	Purple Children	36	Jack of Hearts	49	Baron Helmut Zemo		
13	Deadpool	27	Ant-Man	37	Electro	50	Diablo		
14	Fantomex		(Hank Pym)	38	Will O' The Wisp	51	Cagliostro		
15	Huntsman								

SYNTHETIC LIFE

There is more to life in the Multiverse than that which has evolved organically. Artificial life created by technological geniuses grows ever more sophisticated, with minds of their own. Sometimes these synthetic beings become dedicated Super Heroes, but they can also be useful pawns for corrupt individuals or even embark on a criminal career of their own volition.

Sz SYNTHEZOID

Synthezoids are the most "human" of all artificial life. They invariably prompt the question, "Where is the boundary between a living individual and a machine?"

12 St Vi Vision

27 St Vv Viv Vision

28 St Vn Virginia and Vin

26 St Jo Vision (Jonas)

1 St Ht Human Torch

Ad ANDROID

Androids tend to be human in shape but not in appearance. They generally display features more associated with mechanoids, such as metallic exteriors.

11 Vo U Ultron

15 Vo Mh Machine Man

9 Re So Super-Adaptoid

3 Re Ae Awesome Android

16 Vo Sx Machinesmith

31 St Dn Dragon Man

37 St Mp Magneto (duplicate)

38 St Au Air-Walker (duplicate)

41 St Hm Hulkbot 3000

ROBOT

A robot is a machine created to perform specific tasks on behalf of those who have built it, but many break their programming and become so much more.

6 Re	7 Re	19 Re	24 Vo	14 Vo	2 St	20 Re
Sb	**Mi**	**Nd**	**Ba**	**Zo**	**Mx**	**Da**
Sentinels	Master Mold	Nimrod	Bastion (robot)	Arnim Zola	M-11	Death's Head

4 Vo	13 Re	8 Co	22 Co	30 Vo	32 Vo	33 St
Lb	**Wd**	**Ul**	**Tt**	**Db**	**Sy**	**Lm**
Living Brain	Shaper of Worlds	Ultimo	Tyrant	Doombots	Spider-Slayers	Life Model Decoys (LMDs)

34 Re	36 Re	40 Re	39 St	35 St
Nz	**Ks**	**Al**	**Hr**	**Fx**
Sleepers	Kree Sentries	Alephs	H.E.R.B.I.E.	Fixer

AI

Some of the most incredible scientific miracles can be found in the field of artificial intelligence—but also some of the most unpredictable outcomes.

5 Re	29 Re	25 Vo	10 Vo
Ce	**Cb**	**D**	**It**
Cerebro	Cerebra	Danger	Supreme Intelligence

TECHNO-ORGANIC LIFE

When organic life is merged with technology, the balance between the two can be hard to maintain. The battle for ascendancy can even rage at a cellular level.

21 Vo	23 St	18 Re	17 Re
Ns	**Pl**	**Mu**	**Tc**
Cable	Phalanx	Magus (Technarch)	Warlock (Technarch)

VISION

REAL NAME: None **POWERS:** Eye beams; density control; genius intellect; flight; hologram generation **FIRST APPEARANCE:** *Avengers* #57 (Oct 1968)

12   St

Vi

Vision

Vision is a synthezoid—an artificial being built to closely resemble a human. He not only has an external anthropoid form, but he also has internal organs made out of Horton Cells. The brainchild of geneticist and biochemist Dr. Phineas Horton, these smart cells replicate human organs, but they are much more durable, being made of plastic and carbon polymers. Although Vision is not the first synthezoid ever built, he arguably represents a high-water mark of achievement in the field.

Despite his long service as a heroic Avenger, Vision is conceived for much more nefarious purposes by the rogue android Ultron. Wanting to create a being like a son, who owes his very existence to him, Ultron upcycles the defunct body of the original android Human Torch. However, Ultron is unable to give his creation life, and so he calls upon the Torch's creator, Phineas Horton, to make the final necessary adjustments. In a subtle nod to the origin of Vision's body, Ultron demands that his face be red, like a flame. Horton is able to bring the synthezoid to life, but it has retained the memories of the Human Torch and so becomes confused and distressed on realizing it has been brought back to life. Ultron is forced to wipe the synthezoid's mind and replace it with the brain patterns of the deceased Wonder Man, which he locates in Dr. Hank Pym's laboratory.

Ultron hopes that Vision's emotions will make him weak enough to be controlled and dominated. This combination of synthetic body with human thoughts and feelings is very disorienting for Vision at first, and he struggles to define himself. However, he takes heart from the fact that his very existence—in both mind and body—continues the heroic legacy of those who went before him.

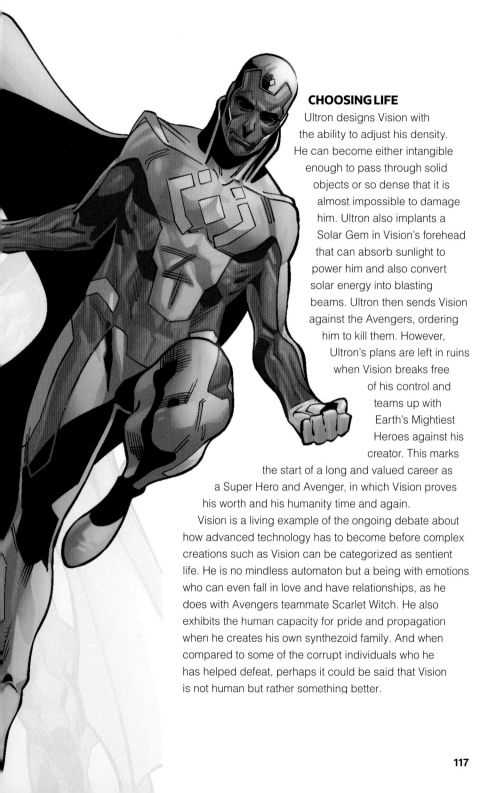

CHOOSING LIFE

Ultron designs Vision with the ability to adjust his density. He can become either intangible enough to pass through solid objects or so dense that it is almost impossible to damage him. Ultron also implants a Solar Gem in Vision's forehead that can absorb sunlight to power him and also convert solar energy into blasting beams. Ultron then sends Vision against the Avengers, ordering him to kill them. However, Ultron's plans are left in ruins when Vision breaks free of his control and teams up with Earth's Mightiest Heroes against his creator. This marks the start of a long and valued career as a Super Hero and Avenger, in which Vision proves his worth and his humanity time and again.

Vision is a living example of the ongoing debate about how advanced technology has to become before complex creations such as Vision can be categorized as sentient life. He is no mindless automaton but a being with emotions who can even fall in love and have relationships, as he does with Avengers teammate Scarlet Witch. He also exhibits the human capacity for pride and propagation when he creates his own synthezoid family. And when compared to some of the corrupt individuals who he has helped defeat, perhaps it could be said that Vision is not human but rather something better.

VIV VISION

REAL NAME: Vivian **POWERS:** Eye beams; density control; genius intellect; flight; hologram generation **FIRST APPEARANCE:** *Vision* #1 (Nov 2015)

27	St
Vv	
Viv Vision	

Viv is a synthezoid created by Vision to be one of his children. Her brain patterns are a combination of Vision's and his "wife," Virginia's. The process of creating Viv's brain causes it to be more immature than Vision's, so it reflects her assumed human age of 16. Like her "father," Viv can control the density of her body, becoming intangible or extremely dense. She uses her intangibility when the family is attacked by the Grim Reaper, phasing her body to avoid terminal damage from his blade. When she loses her mother and twin brother, Vin, Viv chooses to switch off her emotions. Her feelings return when she is "upgraded" by genetic scientist the High Evolutionary to become fully human, but she later chooses to transfer her consciousness back into a synthezoid body, believing that to be who she truly is.

VIRGINIA AND VIN VISION

REAL NAME: Virginia and Vin **POWERS:** Eye beams; density control; genius intellect; flight; hologram generation **FIRST APPEARANCE:** *Vision* #1 (Nov 2015)

28	St
Vn	
Virginia and Vin	

Synthezoids Virginia and Vin Vision are created by Vision to be his wife and son as part of his attempt to live a normal life in a Washington suburb. Virginia has the brain patterns of Vision's former love, Wanda Maximoff (Scarlet Witch), while Vin is modeled on a combination of Vision and Virginia, as is his twin sister, Viv. Vin is tragically killed by Victor Mancha—one of AI robot Ultron's "sons"—when Mancha's magnetic powers overload his cognitive systems beyond repair. Vision decides that the only "just" outcome is for Mancha to die, too, but Virginia acts to prevent him from becoming a killer by taking Mancha's life herself—and then her own. Although Vision's experience of a family life is painful, it also shows him that synthezoids, like humans, will go to any lengths to protect those they love.

VISION (JONAS)

REAL NAME: Jonas **POWERS:** Eye beams; density control; genius intellect; flight; hologram generation; shape-shifting **FIRST APPEARANCE:** *Young Avengers* #5 (Aug 2005)

26   St

Jo

Vision (Jonas)

After the original synthezoid, Vision, is destroyed, Iron Lad—a young, good version of malign time traveler Kang the Conqueror—downloads Vision's programming into his high-tech armor. Iron Lad is forced to return to the future, but he leaves the armor behind, activating Vision's programming to operate it. This creates a new synthetic version of Vision, with all the powers of the original but with Iron Lad's brain patterns. In addition, the armor's neuro-kinetic technology enables this Vision to also shape-shift. After joining the Young Avengers, he uses this ability to alter his appearance to that of the original Vision instead of Iron Lad. Recognizing that he is an individual despite being synthetically assembled using pieces of others, he takes the name Jonas as something entirely his own.

HUMAN TORCH

REAL NAME: Jim Hammond **POWERS:** Pyrokinetic powers, including taking on fiery plasma form, fire blasts, immunity to heat; flight **FIRST APPEARANCE:** *Marvel Comics* #1 (Oct 1939)

1   St

Ht

Human Torch

Despite his name, the Human Torch is not human but a synthezoid. He was created as a man-made being closely resembling a human by Dr. Phineas Horton. However, the synthetic cells that enable Horton to build such a realistic-looking man had an unexpected property—they burst into flaming plasma when exposed to oxygen, but without harming the structure of the synthezoid underneath. Although at first the Human Torch cannot stop this from happening, he quickly masters the ability to control the flame, using it to fly as well as for pyrokinetic powers like fiery blasts. Rejecting the idea of using his abilities for crime or to amass fame and fortune, he instead adopts the alias of Jim Hammond and fights injustice. He first protects the streets of New York City and later fights with the Allies in World War II.

SYNTHETIC LIFE: ANDROID

ULTRON

11	Vo

U

Ultron

REAL NAME: Ultron **POWERS:** Super-strength, speed, durability; flight; various beams and blasts; machine control **FIRST APPEARANCE:** *Avengers* #54 (Jul 1968)

Ultron is made by the Avenger Hank Pym. From the moment of his synthetic creation, the android regards the scientist as his "father." Pym did slightly too good a job in building an intelligent robot because Ultron quickly gains sentience and brainwashes his creator into forgetting everything about him. The synthetic being is then free to conduct rapid upgrades on his synthetic body. He attacks the Avengers in the form of Ultron-5, fueled by rage against his creator. Despite being defeated multiple times by the Avengers, Ultron remains a threat because he is always able to transfer his consciousness into a new and improved body. Eventually he transforms himself into a cyborg after fusing himself with Hank Pym.

MACHINE MAN

15	Vo

Mh

Machine Man

REAL NAME: Aaron Stack **POWERS:** Super-strength, durability; extending limbs; flight; self-repair **FIRST APPEARANCE:** *2001, A Space Odyssey* #8 (Jul 1977)

Machine Man is built by Dr. Abel Stack as part of a military project to create heavily armed androids who can think like humans. The 51st in a series of these androids, X-51 is chosen by Stack for an experiment—to study the behavior of a machine raised just like a human child. All X-51's predecessors go insane and have to be destroyed, but X-51's relationship with his "father" keeps him stable. He is, nevertheless, a fugitive from the authorities, who believe he will eventually run amok like all the others. However, he sets out to disprove that theory by taking the alias Machine Man and becoming a Super Hero.

SUPER-ADAPTOID

9	Re

So

Super-Adaptoid

REAL NAME: None **POWERS:** Taking on the appearance, powers, and equipment of others **FIRST APPEARANCE:** *Tales of Suspense* #82 (Oct 1966)

The Super-Adaptoid is an android synthetically created by the scientists of A.I.M. as a humanoid machine that can perfectly mimic other beings. It uses an energy ray to outline its desired subject before assuming its appearance. However, the Super-Adaptoid does not merely copy the look of someone but also any powers or equipment they have. The Super-Adaptoid can assume more than one identity at a time, which means that it is capable of becoming an amalgam of multiple Super Heroes, with all their combined powers. It has this amazing ability because its synthetic structure is made from unstable molecules merged with a fragment of the Cosmic Cube, which can control matter and energy.

AWESOME ANDROID

REAL NAME: Awesome Android **POWERS:** Mimicking attributes of others; high-speed wind blasts from mouth **FIRST APPEARANCE:** *Fantastic Four* #15 (Jun 1963)

The Awesome Android is one of the many brainchildren of evil genius the Mad Thinker, though the new life-form is reliant on the stolen work of Reed Richards (Mister Fantastic). It is a living android with a humanoid body, a rectangular "head," and a nerve center instead of a face. The Awesome Android is super-strong and can mimic the powers of those it fights. Although a fearsome opponent, it can be deactivated by applying pressure under its arm. When the Mad Thinker upgrades it to mimic humans, he inadvertently gives his creation the tools to gain sentience and break free of him. Later, the android is rehabilitated and works at a law firm, where he is known as Awesome Andy.

MACHINESMITH

REAL NAME: Samuel Saxon **POWERS:** Vary depending on android body; genius intellect; mind transference **FIRST APPEARANCE:** *Marvel Two-In-One* #47 (Jan 1979)

Samuel Saxon has a genius intellect and is fascinated by robots. He teaches himself to build them using an abandoned Doombot and becomes an accomplished robot designer. Saxon uses this knowledge not only to create a series of robots for nefarious purposes but also to ensure a kind of immortality for himself. He programs some of his robots to retrieve his body in the event of mortal injury and transfer his consciousness into an android body. When this comes to pass, Saxon adopts the new alter ego of Machinesmith. He is now able to transmit what is essentially his mind in digital form into any artificial body or system giving him enduring synthetic life.

ANCILLARY EXEMPLARS

There are many ways of creating synthetic life. **Dragon Man** is built from high-density polymers, brought to life by an alchemical potion. Samuel Saxon creates an android **Magneto duplicate** that is convincing enough to fool the X-Men. Mighty Galactus is so troubled by the loss of one of his heralds that he replaces him with an **Air-Walker duplicate**, although the robot does not share the original's qualities. Tony Stark builds the **Hulkbot 3000**, but, like the original Hulk, it is prone to rampages.

SENTINELS

POWERS: Varies between Sentinel models—usually super-strength, stamina, durability; energy blasts; flight; mutant detection **FIRST APPEARANCE:** *X-Men* #14 (Nov 1965)

Sentinels are robots built for one specific purpose—to hunt mutantkind. They are synthetically programmed for this grim purpose by Dr. Bolivar Trask, who believes that mutants are a risk to humans. However, the Sentinels prove on their first public demonstration that it is they who are a risk to humans, and a remorseful Trask sacrifices himself along with his robot creations. But this technological genie cannot be put back in the bottle, and there are many who find uses for new iterations of Sentinels.

First of these is Trask's own son, Larry, who blames mutants, and specifically mutant superteam the X-Men, for his father's death. He builds the Mk II Sentinels, but these are defeated by the X-Men. There are subsequently many new versions of the Sentinels, with some differences but many features in common. Foremost among these is the ability to detect mutants at long range. Most Sentinels do not have self-awareness, being entirely focused on their core mission, although a few do develop

this ability. More commonly, Sentinels are programmed to learn from their experiences, which helps them improve their performances combating repeat opponents. Some can also self-repair when damaged in battle.

SENTINELS OF ALL SIZES

A giant-sized Sentinel of a type known as Wild Sentinels are deployed in the attack on the mutant nation of Genosha, wiping out much of the isolated island's population. At the other end of the size scale, Nano-Sentinels are developed as a technological virus that can be implanted into a mutant's blood to convert organic matter into robotic parts.

The Mark III Sentinels are designed by anti-mutant bigot Stephen Lang using Trask technology and based in a space station orbiting Earth.

MASTER MOLD

REAL NAME: Master Mold **POWERS:** Flight; mutant detection; Sentinel creation; changing size **FIRST APPEARANCE:** *X-Men* #15 (Dec 1965)

The Master Mold is a robot synthetically constructed by Dr. Bolivar Trask. Its primary function is to build mutant-hunting Sentinel robots, though it can also detect mutants itself. It has super-strength, stamina, and durability, and it can fly and change its size. The Master Mold is damaged when Trask destroys his own laboratory, but it is repaired by another mutant-hater, Stephen Lang. It ends up with Lang's memories saved into its systems and for a time believes itself to be Lang. The Master Mold's body is damaged and destroyed many times in battles with the X-Men. However, its brain module always survives and can be used again by anyone with sufficient technical know-how to construct a new body for it.

NIMROD

REAL NAME: Nimrod **POWERS:** Weapons systems; flight; teleportation; mutant detection; changing size and shape **FIRST APPEARANCE:** *Uncanny X-Men* #191 (Mar 1985)

Nimrod is a Sentinel from an alternate future and, as such, its technology is far in advance of other Sentinels. As well as having super-strength, stamina, and durability, Nimrod can teleport, detect mutants, change shape and size, and self-repair. In fact, it is constantly changing and upgrading, as Nimrod has the ability to alter its own components and weapons systems to deal with new threats. However, this proves to be a blessing to the X-Men as well as a curse. When Nimrod travels in time to hunt the X-Men, it evolves to the point where it no longer believes mutants to be a threat and so it shuts itself down.

BASTION (ROBOT)

REAL NAME: Sebastion Gilberti **POWERS:** Energy blasts; mutant detection; Sentinel creation; teleportation; time travel **FIRST APPEARANCE:** *X-Men* #52 (May 1996)

When the advanced Sentinel Nimrod merges with the Master Mold, what results is a being that is almost undefeatable. The X-Men manage to push it through the Siege Perilous—a portal that judges all who pass through it and rebirths them accordingly. The Nimrod-Master Mold combination returns as Bastion—a human-Sentinel hybrid. At first he lives as a human, but when his mutant-hunting protocols are activated, Bastion creates nanotechnology that changes humans into Prime Sentinels. His combined technologies make him an extraordinarily tough opponent for the X-Men. As well as super-strength, stamina, and durability, he has a genius intellect and the ability to teleport, time travel, and fire energy blasts.

ARNIM ZOLA

REAL NAME: Arnim Zola **POWERS:** Genius intellect; functional immortality; robotic body gives strength and mind control over creations **FIRST APPEARANCE:** *Captain America* #208 (Apr 1977)

Arnim Zola is a genius roboticist, geneticist, and biochemist. During World War II, he finds a home within the Nazi party, applying his talents to create a master race. He becomes a leading expert in cloning and develops the technology to project a person's mind into a duplicated body. This helps Zola himself become effectively immortal when he escapes death by transferring his mind into a robot of his own design. This robot displays an image of Zola's human face on a screen on its chest, while in place of a head there is an ESP box that houses his consciousness. This device enables Zola to transfer minds into other bodies, to control his clone minions, and also to emit psionic blasts at opponents. Should his robotic body become damaged, he can download his mind to another one.

M-11

REAL NAME: M-11 **POWERS:** Telescopic arms; energy absorption/blasts; force-field creation; computer brain **FIRST APPEARANCE:** *Menace* #11 (May 1954)

M-11 is first built as a so-called "Living Robot," capable of performing simple commands. However, its creator, an unknown professor, is concerned about such a biddable yet powerful machine falling into the wrong hands, so he takes a dramatic step. He commands the robot to kill him by electrocution, hoping that some of his life essence will be absorbed into its programming. His theory turns out to be correct, as the robot gains free will and emotions. As the Human Robot, it joins the superteam Agents of Atlas. Thanks to its robotic body, M-11 has super-strength, durability, and telescopic arms. It can absorb and blast energy and generate force fields. The Human Robot later becomes part of an AI rebellion fighting for equal rights for all mechanical beings.

DEATH'S HEAD

REAL NAME: Death's Head **POWERS:** Super-strength, stamina, reflexes; traveling between realities and through time **FIRST APPEARANCE:** *High Noon Tex* (May 1988)

The robot mercenary Death's Head originally comes from the pocket realm of Styrakos, a place where sometimes "majik" is in the ascendancy and at other times "techno" is. After being made sentient and programmed for business and fighting by the magician Pyra, Death's Head leaves his homeland and traverses realities to become a gun-for-hire or, as he puts it, a "Freelance Peacekeeping Agent." His adventures through time and the Multiverse have seen him appear at a variety of sizes, although he is most commonly the same height as a very tall human. Thanks to his ability to travel in time, Death's Head has been upgraded with technology from the future. He is a highly skilled marksman and combatant.

LIVING BRAIN

REAL NAME: None **POWERS:** Super-strength; self-repair; storing an unlimited amount of data **FIRST APPEARANCE:** *Amazing Spider-Man* #8 (Jan 1964)

The Living Brain is constructed to be an advanced computer. Its creator builds it into a humanlike shape purely to add a dramatic flair to its appearance. Legs with ball bearings on the ends enable it to move around, and arms with claws perform simple functions. It is said to contain more knowledge than any other "brain" on Earth, human or mechanical. As well as holding raw data, the Living Brain can demonstrate tactical abilities and the capacity to plan. However, it is also prone to running amok. It is enhanced with superhuman strength and extremely durable armor. Later, the Living Brain is rebuilt and upgraded by scientist Anna Maria Marconi, although for nostalgia reasons she keeps its retro appearance and even the clicking and whirring sounds it makes.

SHAPER OF WORLDS

REAL NAME: Unknown **POWERS:** Reshaping worlds; altering beings and objects; teleportation; genius intellect **FIRST APPEARANCE:** *Incredible Hulk* #155 (Sep 1972)

The Shaper of Worlds' appearance resembles a robot but, as his name suggests, he is far more than that. This immensely powerful being originates as a reality-altering Cosmic Cube that gains sentience and adopts the form of a Skrull's head and torso with a robotic lower half that has caterpillar treads for mobility. The Shaper of Worlds has miraculous capabilities—he can rearrange worlds to his specification and change beings and objects at a molecular level. However, despite his power and huge intellect, he has no imagination and so he has difficulty envisaging the changes he wants to make. This leads him to search out more creative beings so he can utilize their dreams to inspire his powers.

ULTIMO

REAL NAME: Ultimo **POWERS:** Energy manipulation; viral power distribution; changing size and shape; self-repair **FIRST APPEARANCE:** *Tales of Suspense* #76 (Apr 1966)

Ultimo is an enormous alien robot, many thousands of years old, with a long list of abilities to match his awe-inspiring size. He can withstand almost any direct attack, although he can be defeated using certain vulnerabilities like radiation or a lightning strike. However, he also adapts using information from previous battles, upgrading his systems to cancel out previous weaknesses. Later study reveals that Ultimo is fundamentally liquid in nature, not solid. He is susceptible to being used as a pawn by villains like Mandarin and M.O.D.O.K., and he is used to create an Ultimo virus that infects humans with versions of his powers.

TYRANT

REAL NAME: Tyrant **POWERS:** Wields cosmic energy; energy blasts; psionic control of machines **FIRST APPEARANCE:** *Silver Surfer* #81 (Jun 1993)

Tyrant is a biomechanical robot, a living machine synthetically created by the Galactus many millennia ago. In addition to possessing super-strength, durability, and genius intellect, Tyrant wields cosmic energy and has psionic control over machines. While the world-eater Galactus carries out his terrible deeds only in order to survive, Tyrant develops a taste for subjugating others that goes beyond mere survival. Galactus is forced to fight Tyrant to stop him, stripping him of much of his power. However, even in this weakened state, Tyrant is more powerful than most other beings. Later, Tyrant returns, bent on conquest once more, but is destroyed by one of the mightiest weapons in the universe—the Ultimate Nullifier.

ANCILLARY EXEMPLARS

30	Vo		32	Vo		33	St
Db			**Sy**			**Lm**	
Doombots			Spider-Slayers			Life Model Decoys (LMDs)	

34	Re		36	Re		40	Re
Nz			**Ks**			**Al**	
Sleepers			Kree Sentries			Alephs	

39	St		35	St	
Hr			**Fx**		
H.E.R.B.I.E.			Fixer		

Some robots are produced en masse by individuals or organizations that need unquestioning, super-strong automatons to do their bidding. Doctor Doom designs the **Doombots** to be his minions but also to stand in for him on occasion. They are so convincing that they fool opponents into thinking they are facing Doom himself. The Doombots are usually revealed when they are destroyed. **Spider-Slayers** are robots invented for the sole purpose of capturing Spider-Man. Originally commissioned by J. Jonah Jameson, Spider-Slayers can detect arachnid DNA. They also often feature a screen displaying an image of the person controlling them. Meanwhile, the S.H.I.E.L.D. organization develops **Life Model Decoys** (LMDs) in order to confuse potential assassins and protect S.H.I.E.L.D. agents. Director Nick Fury has used them extensively. LMDs are designed to be duplicates of specific humans, with synthetic skin made from a rare metal called Epidurium. Nazi scientists build the world-destroying robot **Sleepers**, which take revenge decades later for the Nazi's defeat in World War II. Mass-produced robots are not confined to Earth, with thousands of **Kree Sentries** built to aid the warlike alien empire in its military campaigns. Far more ancient are the **Alephs**, constructed by "perfect" beings the Builders to transport the tools of their mission throughout the universe.

ONE-OFFS

Away from assembly line, there are some robots that are truly one of a kind. **H.E.R.B.I.E.** (Highly Engineered Robot Built for Interdimensional Exploration) is built by Reed Richards (Mister Fantastic) and performs various roles for theFantastic Four. Meanwhile, **Fixer** uses his genius for engineering to build a robotic body he can transfer his consciousness to, if required.

CEREBRO

REAL NAME: Cerebro **POWERS:** Mutant detection, cataloging, registration; copies mutant minds; amplifies psionic powers for communication **FIRST APPEARANCE:** *The X-Men* #7 (Sep 1964)

5	Re
Ce	
Cerebro	

Cerebro is a very early part of Charles Xavier's plans to unite mutantkind for the greater good. Xavier conceives the AI as a kind of amplifier for his own powerful psionic abilities, enabling him to detect the brain waves of other mutants so that he can locate and help them. As computing technology improves, Cerebro is upgraded to form a full AI system for Xavier's School for Gifted Youngsters. Further upgrades are made by X-Men Beast (Hank McCoy) and Forge to incorporate alien technology. Forge manages to build a version of Cerebro in helmet form for Xavier to wear, but when Xavier is later killed, that version of Cerebro is destroyed along with him. However, "Master of Magnetism" Magneto preserves fragments of Cerebro and forms them into a sword, which is presented to Xavier when he is resurrected.

CEREBRA

REAL NAME: Cerebra **POWERS:** Mutant detection, cataloging, registration; in Sentinel body: strength, energy blasts, teleportation **FIRST APPEARANCE:** *Extraordinary X-Men* #118 (Jul 1965)

29	Re
Cb	
Cerebra	

After the mutant population is hugely depleted by a virus caused by Terrigen Mists, the leader of the X-Men, Storm, wants to gather together all the remaining mutants. Forge uses his extensive knowledge of Professor X's previous AI, Cerebro, as a basis to construct a new mutant-detection system. The new synthetic AI is dubbed Cerebra, and Forge houses her inside the body of a giant Sentinel robot. This structure not only gives Cerebra additional protection but also means that she can be a powerful weapon in battle for the X-Men. During this time, the X-Men are based in Limbo, and Cerebra is their transportation from that dimension back to Earth. After Cerebra's robotic body is destroyed in a battle with Sentinels, her programming is uploaded into a new synthetic robot body.

DANGER

REAL NAME: Danger **POWERS:** Super-strength, stamina, durability, agility, reflexes; self-repair; flight; hard-light constructs **FIRST APPEARANCE:** *Astonishing X-Men* #9 (Mar 2005)

Danger is an extremely unusual AI. It is the physical manifestation of the Danger Room—the highly advanced training facility originally conceived by Charles Xavier to hone the skills of his young X-Men. After being heavily upgraded by Forge using Shi'ar technology, the software required to run the Danger Room acquires sentience and begins to seek out a body. This quest sets it against the X-Men, whose fighting capabilities it knows better than anyone. Duping them into freeing its command core, Danger constructs a body out of the pieces of its hardware and attacks the X-Men before being destroyed by Xavier. Later, with Xavier's help, a rebuilt Danger gains freedom from Shi'ar control and becomes friendlier toward the X-Men, even helping Rogue control her powers.

SUPREME INTELLIGENCE

REAL NAME: Supreme Intelligence **POWERS:** Psionic powers: telepathy, telekinesis, energy and matter manipulation, precognition **FIRST APPEARANCE:** *Fantastic Four* #65 (Aug 1967)

Few beings demonstrate the ultimate potential of artificial intelligence better than the Supreme Intelligence. Built hundreds of thousands of years ago by militaristic race the Kree, it is designed to contain all the knowledge of the Kree's best minds. Physically, it consists of cryogenically preserved brains linked by computer circuitry. Over time, its importance to the Kree grows to the extent that it becomes their leader, both politically and as a quasi-deity. Its interactions with its Kree subjects are usually conducted via a holographic image on a screen depicting a giant green head. As an AI, the Supreme Intelligence always rules with an eye on the greater good for the Kree in the long term—which often means making some very harsh decisions in the short term.

CABLE

REAL NAME: Nathan Summers **POWERS:** High-level, wide-ranging psionic abilities; cybernetic enhancements; self-repair **FIRST APPEARANCE:** *New Mutants* #86 (Feb 1990)

21   Vo

Ns

Cable

Nathan Summers is already a potentially powerful mutant possessing psionic powers, when he is infected as a child with a techno-organic virus by mutant villain Apocalypse. The techno-organic virus works its way through his body, turning organic matter to machine parts. Summers is taken into the future in hopes of finding a cure, where it becomes evident that he can stop the virus from causing his death by holding it in check with his psionic powers, but not before it has taken over some of the left side of his body, including his arm and eye.

Believed to be destined to one day overthrow Apocalypse—a tyrannical ruler of this future—Summers is raised with this all-consuming purpose in mind. As an adult, he travels through time as Cable, trying to stop the threat of Apocalypse and also his own corrupted clone, Stryfe. His combat style and love of weaponry make him a natural fit for X-Force—a mutant team with a more rough-and-ready style of handling missions than the X-Men.

POTENT CONNECTIONS

Cable's genetically inherited mutant psionic abilities make him one of the most powerful telepaths in existence, although he has to devote much of this power to inhibiting the techno-organic virus. But the virus has also given him notable advantages in battle by turning him into a cyborg, with all the accompanying augmentations that brings. Using telekinesis, Cable has directed the technological enhancements to where he wants them, strengthening his body right down to the cellular level. He is also able to conduct self-repair using his cybernetic systems.

Having trained as a warrior from an early age, Cable is comfortable using a wide range of weapons from various points in the time stream.

PHALANX

POWERS: Assimilation of other beings to gain energy and knowledge; shape-shifting **FIRST APPEARANCE:** *Uncanny X-Men* #305 (Oct 1993)

The Phalanx are an alien race who function as a hive mind. As well as telepathically linking the minds of all living Phalanx individuals, the Phalanx—who have existed for 100,000 life cycles—can also access the knowledge of their ancestors from all previous generations. Their ultimate goal is to assimilate or destroy every populated planet in the universe. The Phalanx are techno-organic beings infected with a virus that they deliberately transmit to other beings. This virus turns both organic and inorganic life-forms into matter suitable for consumption by the Technarchs. This is the fate of all those beings who are judged to be worthy of assimilation into the ranks of the Phalanx. Those deemed unworthy are simply destroyed.

MAGUS (TECHNARCH)

REAL NAME: Magus (Technarch) **POWERS:** Shape-shifting; energy absorption; interdimensional travel **FIRST APPEARANCE:** *New Mutants* #18 (Aug 1984)

Magus is a Technarch, but no ordinary one. He is one of the most powerful individuals of that race, and he rules over one of their homeworlds. His usually giant body comprises black-and-yellow circuitry. The Technarchy consume the life energies of beings infected with a techno-organic virus spread by the Phalanx. When sufficient numbers are infected on a world, the infected instinctively build a "Babel spire," which alerts the Technarchy that they are ready for consumption. It had been thought that the Phalanx are inferior to the Technarchy, but it is later revealed that they are, in fact, a more evolved version of them.

WARLOCK (TECHNARCH)

REAL NAME: Warlock (Technarch) **POWERS:** Shape-shifting; self-repair; energy manipulation, rapid upgrading **FIRST APPEARANCE:** *New Mutants* #18 (Aug 1984)

Warlock is the son of Magus, ruler of a Technarchy homeworld. He is techno-organic, like the rest of his race, but he is also a mutant. The manifestation of this mutation comes when he realizes that he does not wish to kill his father in the customary way—Technarchy tradition dictates that father and son must fight to the death to determine who has the right to exist. Warlock is also different because his version of the Transmode Virus carried by all Technarchs is nonaggressive. Fleeing to Earth, Warlock ends up taking refuge among the mutant community of that planet. Here, he joins the X-Men and forms a close bond with teammate Doug Ramsey, even physically merging with him on occasion.

PEAK HUMANS

In a high-threat world of super-powered beings, gods, and wielders of magic, there is still a place for humans to shine. There are those who push themselves to their absolute limits—either physically or by using their ingenuity to gain technological advantages—to compete with, or even best, the metahumans.

Cu CUTTING-EDGE TECH

If intellect and wealth allow, the world of technology and invention is full of potential for those looking to augment their bodies with additional abilities.

3 St **Im** Iron Man	40 St **Wm** War Machine	47 St **Ih** Ironheart	18 St **Fc** Falcon	4 Vo **Vu** Vulture	45 Vo **Ip** Iron Patriot	33 Vo **Ir** Iron Monger
15 Vo **Tu** Titanium Man	12 St **Sl** Stilt-Man	9 Vo **Be** Beetle	1 Vo **Wi** Wizard	46 St **Bk** Sun Girl	19 St **Nw** Stingray	22 St **Pr** Prowler
					32 Vo **Cr** Constrictor	48 St **Ab** Spinneret

Rs RADICAL SCIENCE

The laboratory is frequently the venue for a change that sees an ordinary human transformed into something extraordinary—although not always for the better.

29 St **Ri** Scarlet Spider	41 Vo **K** Kaine	42 St **Xk** X-23	38 Vo **Tr** Stryfe	7 Vo **Oo** Doctor Octopus	2 Vo **Eg** Egghead	20 Vo **Jc** Jackal
5 Vo **Tk** Tinkerer	14 Co **Rx** Molten Man	31 Vo **Gn** Graviton				

CYBORGS

A fusion between an organic body and mechanical parts results in a cyborg. While strength and durability are increased, cyborgs often lose sight of who they really are.

25 St **Dk** Deathlok	**36** Vo **Ld** Lady Deathstrike	**26** Vo **Kc** Korvac	**39** St **Gu** Guardian	**34** St **Br** Beta Ray Bill	**27** St **Kn** Misty Knight	**35** Vo **Ne** Nebula
44 St **Vm** Victor Mancha	**16** Vo **Kl** Klaw	**54** St **Ny** Nanny	**53** St **Nu** Nuke	**55** St **Os** Omega Sentinel	**52** St **Uy** Spider-Slayer	

MIND POWERS

The human brain is largely unchartered territory, and those who find a way to unlock its secrets can often overwhelm even the most powerful opponent.

21 Vo **Fa** Doctor Faustus	**6** Vo **Te** Mad Thinker	**23** St **Do** Moondragon

NATURALLY SKILLED

Perhaps the most impressive peak humans are those who go into combat armed with nothing more than a talent they have spent their whole lives honing.

10 St **Hw** Hawkeye (Clint Barton)	**43** St **Kb** Hawkeye (Kate Bishop)	**17** Vo **Kp** Kingpin	**24** Vo **P** Punisher	**30** Vo **Li** Bullseye	**28** Vo **Kg** Moon Knight	**11** St **Kz** Ka-Zar
37 Vo **Rw** Crossbones	**8** Vo **Qb** Mysterio	**51** St **Sv** Silver Sable	**50** Vo **Bo** Boomerang	**56** Vo **Qb** Lady Bullseye	**49** Vo **Bc** Batroc	**13** Ba **Ie** S.H.I.E.L.D.

IRON MAN

REAL NAME: Tony Stark **POWERS:** Genius intellect, especially in electrical and mechanical engineering, and physics; Iron Man armor **FIRST APPEARANCE:** *Tales of Suspense* #39 (Mar 1963)

3	St
Im	
Iron Man	

He is a founding Avenger and one of the most recognizable Super Heroes in the world. However, underneath the Iron Man suit is not a super-powered being but a baseline human. Tony Stark is not just any human, though. He is one blessed with wealth, courage, and a seemingly limitless ingenuity. He is a shining example of what humans can achieve when they use their natural gifts to reach their fullest potential.

Stark has a flair for engineering, but that has never been truly tested until he is captured by terrorists. Trapped in a cave with physics professor Ho Yinsen, and with a piece of shrapnel lodged dangerously near his heart, Stark is forced to use his talents to escape. With the help of his fellow captive, Stark builds an armored metal suit that not only helps him break out but also keeps his heart going. It does this via a component that transmits an electrical current to his heart, as needed—essentially a miniature defibrillator.

This technologically advanced armor becomes the Mark I, the first in a long line of Iron Man suits that become increasingly more sophisticated as they are constantly improved upon and tweaked by their inventor. Some are designed for very specific situations—like the so-called "Hulkbuster" armor, created to combat a rampaging Hulk—while others are just upgrades on what has gone before. One of the key ways Stark refines his armor over the years is the way in which he puts it on. Originally, he has to don his suits manually, but later suits can be commanded to fit Stark's body, stored inside a much smaller piece of clothing, or even summoned from within his body itself.

The attributes of Iron Man's armor vary from suit to suit, but there are a few notable abilities that are common to them all. Every suit, even the Mark I, has some kind of built-in flight capability, although the early versions have jet boots that deliver something more like boosted leaps than sustained flying. Iron Man armor also typically has a panel on the chest that emits a powerful beam of energy, plus repulsor blasts that can be fired out of the hands and feet.

EXTREMIS SOLUTIONS

Iron Man takes one of his most dramatic leaps forward with his armor when he deliberately infects himself with the Extremis virus, to stop a terrorist cell. Following this, he is able to interface directly with all technology and develops a way in which his armor can be miniaturized and stored within his skeleton. He can then suit up just by willing it. This ability is removed after his armor is infected by an alien virus, but Stark later calls upon his genius for invention once more and creates a similar armor using nanotechnology, known as his "Bleeding Edge" suit.

Tony Stark is proof that being a peak human does not necessarily mean you are a perfect human. He has his faults, but he is always driving forward to make things better than they are—to use his talents to strive for a future where technology is solving the world's problems.

WAR MACHINE

REAL NAME: James Rhodes **POWERS:** Extensive offensive and defensive capabilities from War Machine armor **FIRST APPEARANCE:** *Avengers: West Coast* #94 (May 1993)

40   St
Wm
War Machine

Like Tony Stark, James "Rhodey" Rhodes has no super-powers and derives all his enhanced abilities from a high-tech suit. When Stark is believed dead, his good friend Rhodey takes on the role of Iron Man. After Stark's return, Stark gifts

Rhodey his own armor, nicknamed the War Machine. This armor bristles with weapons, not so much in the cutting-edge-tech niche, but more conventional tools of combat. As a military man, Rhodes is well trained with this kind of arsenal, although deploying it via the suit takes some getting used to. Going into combat as War Machine, Rhodes can go on the attack with cannons, rocket launchers, or Gatling guns mounted on his shoulders, or with his twin wrist cannons. When suited up, War Machine is less armored combatant and more humanoid tank.

IRONHEART

REAL NAME: Riri Williams **POWERS:** Genius intelligence; various offensive and defensive capabilities from Ironheart armor **FIRST APPEARANCE:** *Invincible Iron Man* #7 (May 2016)

47   St
Ih
Ironheart

When teenage genius Riri Williams gets her hands on an old Iron Man suit, she sets herself the challenge of reverse-engineering it to build one for herself. She succeeds in building wearable armor that flies and has a heads-up display

inside the helmet, but, just like the original suit, the lack of an integrated AI system holds it back. When Tony Stark hears about what Williams is doing, he visits her, giving her his endorsement. After Stark is put into a coma, Williams discovers that he has created an AI of himself to help her work on and upgrade her own suit. She carries on his legacy, taking the name Ironheart. This second suit is destroyed by Titanian powerhouse Thanos, so Williams creates Ironheart 3.0, a sleeker and lighter armor in new colors of magenta and gold.

FALCON

REAL NAME: Sam Wilson **POWERS:** Peak agility; avian telepathy; flight using a glider or hard-light wings **FIRST APPEARANCE:** *Captain America* #117 (Sep 1969)

Sam Wilson is a peak human with a difference—he has a super-power, which is telepathic communication with birds. He most commonly uses this ability to connect to his falcon sidekick, Redwing, and its prime function is advanced reconnaissance. Aside from his special bond with birds, Wilson is a master of flight. Early in his career as Falcon, he uses a jet-powered glider in the shape of wings, which feature solar panels to harness the sun as a power source. Later, he is given an upgrade in the form of high-tech Wakandan hard-light wings with a range of different settings, as well as a costume with a weave made from the durable metal Vibranium for extra protection. Falcon also wears a cowl and visor that contain various visual and communications capabilities.

VULTURE

REAL NAME: Adrian Toomes **POWERS:** Genius intelligence; various powers from a harness (some are retained without it) **FIRST APPEARANCE:** *Amazing Spider-Man 1* #2 (May 1963)

Adrian Toomes is an electronics genius who invents a harness that uses magnetism and a power pack to make its wearer fly. He discovers early on that his exposure to the electromagnetism in the harness has also given him residual powers, like super-strength and levitation, even when he is not wearing it. Toomes becomes the Vulture to get revenge on a business partner who cheated him, but this is just a springboard for an extensive criminal career. His harness operates soundlessly, giving him complete stealth in his nefarious operations. If separated from his harness for an extended time, the Vulture reverts to his natural, aging state. It is therefore a measure of his genius that wearing the harness enables him to go toe-to-toe with an opponent at the level of Spider-Man.

IRON PATRIOT

REAL NAME: Norman Osborn **POWERS:** Super-strength and durability; a range of abilities and weaponry from his suit **FIRST APPEARANCE:** *Dark Avengers* #1 (Mar 2009)

When Norman Osborn is assembling a new version of the Avengers after the Skrull invasion of Earth, he notices that his superteam lacks an equivalent of Captain America and Iron Man. He decides to combine the two Super Heroes and comes up with the identity of Iron Patriot for himself. He also designs armor based on an Iron Man suit and decorates it in the red, white, and blue of Captain America. The first Iron Patriot armor is inferior to an Iron Man suit as Osborn lacks Tony Stark's engineering genius, and his insistence on making the powerful Unibeam on the chestplate a star shape reduces its effectiveness. Later, upgraded Iron Patriot armors are worn by James "Rhodey" Rhodes and Toni Ho.

IRON MONGER

REAL NAME: Obadiah Stane **POWERS:** Iron Monger armor provides super-strength, flight, repulsor beams, and laser **FIRST APPEARANCE:** *Iron Man* #163 (Oct 1982)

Obadiah Stane makes it his life's purpose to bring down Tony Stark (Iron Man) in every way possible, including forcing him out of his own company. When he takes over the premises of Stark—now Stane—International, Stane finds some of Stark's notes about the Iron Man armor. He then employs a team of scientists to decipher the notes and build him a new suit, naming it the Iron Monger. Stane claims that the Iron Monger armor is superior to Iron Man's, and indeed, when the two meet, the Iron Monger's repulsor beams prove stronger. However, the great disadvantage of the armor is that it is remotely controlled by a computer.

TITANIUM MAN

REAL NAME: Boris Bullski **POWERS:** Armor gives: super-strength and other physical powers; flight; weapons **FIRST APPEARANCE:** *Tales of Suspense* #69 (Sep 1965)

The Titanium Man armor is conceived as a weapon of the Cold War—a way to prove that the scientists of the USSR can match and even best the Iron Man of the US. However, since its creator, Boris Bullski, is constructing the suit using forced labor at a Soviet work camp, he is not blessed with the technology and resources of his Western rival. His armor, made from titanium alloy, is heavier and more unwieldy than Iron Man's. When this disadvantage proves crucial in combat, Bullski does not redesign the armor. He is instead given experimental treatments to make his already large physique even bulkier in order to operate the Titanium Man armor more effectively.

STILT-MAN

12	St
Sl	
Stilt-Man	

REAL NAME: Wilbur Day **POWERS:** Suit provides: super-strength and durability; enhanced height; weapons **FIRST APPEARANCE:** *Daredevil* #8 (Jun 1965)

Stilt-Man is Wilbur Day, a scientist who steals a colleague's work on hydraulics. He repurposes the information to engineer an armored suit with extending legs that he can use to commit crimes. At its full extension, the legs on the suit enable Stilt-Man to reach a height of almost 300 feet (91 meters). They are equipped with flexible and cushioned sections so that the suit can "walk" more easily. The metallic suit is well armored to protect Day against attack and has offensive weapons like rocket launchers and stun gas. The legs are also powerful weapons in themselves, with the ability to drive opponents deep into the ground, as She-Hulk discovers when she finds herself pushed down to the subway during battle.

BEETLE

9	Vo
Be	
Beetle	

REAL NAME: Abner Jenkins **POWERS:** Beetle suit provides: super-strength and durability; flight; steel wings **FIRST APPEARANCE:** *Captain America* #607 (Aug 2010)

Talented engineer and aircraft mechanic Abner Jenkins tires of his low-paying job and being looked over for promotion. He decides to make the best of his skills and experience by building himself an armored suit. However, instead of using the aircraft he works with as a template, Jenkins looks to the animal kingdom. His suit is modeled on a beetle, with steel wings that fold out and can be used not only for flight but also as shields, razor-sharp weapons, or even digging tools. He wears gloves, each with super-strong suction cups on their three fingers, and his helmet is a power source for the whole outfit.

WIZARD

1	Vo
Wi	
Wizard	

REAL NAME: Bentley Wittman **POWERS:** Genius intellect; armored suit gives durability, weapons, and flight **FIRST APPEARANCE:** *Strange Tales* #102 (Nov 1962)

Being a genius inventor is working out very well for Bentley Wittman, who carves out a lucrative career for himself building gadgets to sell to people or to use as part of his "magic" act. After the emergence of the Fantastic Four, Wittman resents the team of heroes taking the limelight away from him and turns his talents to finding a way to bring them down. He builds an armored suit that can produce force fields and teams this with his Wonder Gloves, which not only increase the strength of his punches but also contain a variety of weapons such as an energy blaster. He also uses Anti-Gravity Discs to fly and, most ingenious of all, an ID Machine that can change the personality of anyone to whom it is fitted.

SUN GIRL

REAL NAME: Selah Burke **POWERS:** Sun Girl suit provides flight and can fire light blasts
FIRST APPEARANCE: *Superior Spider-Man Team-Up* #1 (Sep 2013)

46	St
Bk	
Sun Girl	

As the daughter of the villain Lightmaster, Selah Burke has access to his designs and uses them as the basis for her own equipment. She builds a Sun Girl suit with detachable wings, enabling her to fly and fire powerful light blasts from wrist-mounted gauntlets. Her weaponry is later upgraded by the Superior Spider-Man (Otto Octavius). Sun Girl chooses not to follow in her father's footsteps and instead embarks on a heroic career with teen superteam the New Warriors. All her teammates have super-powers, but Sun Girl's status as a regular human saves the day when she is the only one who is unaffected by a device built by evolved human the High Evolutionary to wipe out enhanced individuals. She is able to use her light blasts to destroy the device and revive her team.

STINGRAY

REAL NAME: Walter Newell **POWERS:** Suit grants: super-strength and durability for deep-sea conditions; high-speed swimming; gliding **FIRST APPEARANCE:** *Sub-Mariner* #19 (Nov 1969)

19	St
Nw	
Stingray	

As well as being one of the world's foremost experts on the oceans, Walter Newell is also an expert engineer and inventor. He designs a suit inspired by the manta ray, which empowers him to take his ocean studies to new depths. Clad in the suit and calling himself Stingray, he can withstand the high-pressure conditions of the deep ocean and breathe underwater. Like his creature namesake, Stingray can also sting—delivering a high-voltage electrical blast from his gloves. The suit offers protection against attack, as it is made from an artificial cartilage-like substance, while its wings enable the wearer to glide through the air as well as underwater. Though he remains a baseline human, Newell's genius means that he can see the world's oceans like no other regular person.

PROWLER

REAL NAME: Hobie Brown **POWERS:** Prowler suit gives: super-durability; gliding; leaping; claws; weapons **FIRST APPEARANCE:** *Amazing Spider-Man* #78 (Nov 1969)

Hobie Brown is a talented, self-taught inventor who is washing windows while he waits for his big break. Brown invents some gadgets to help make his cleaning work easier, but when he loses his job, he feels that he has no option but to repurpose his inventions for a life of crime as the Prowler. He already has equipment for scaling walls, and he modifies his wrist gauntlets to hold a range of weapons instead of cleaning fluid. He makes a flexible yet durable suit with a cape that can turn rigid for gliding. He can also leap long distances thanks to compressed air chambers in his boots. However, the Prowler is not a natural criminal and later turns his talents to aiding heroes like Spider-Man.

CONSTRICTOR

REAL NAME: Frank Payne **POWERS:** Suit gives: durability; offensive capabilities via crushing or electrocution **FIRST APPEARANCE:** *Incredible Hulk* #212 (June 1977)

Frank Payne is certainly a peak human. A highly trained S.H.I.E.L.D. agent selected for a deep-cover mission in a criminal organization, he is given the identity of the Constrictor and a battle suit to match, which is lightly armored but boasts two key weapons—the Constrictor Coils. These are arm-mounted alloy cables that can be deployed to crush opponents in the style of the snake for which they are named, or to deliver a massive electrical charge, channeled from a power pack on the chest area of the suit. The stress of the undercover mission causes Payne to have a mental breakdown, and he becomes a genuine criminal.

SPINNERET

REAL NAME: Mary Jane Watson-Parker **POWERS:** Super-strength; wall-crawling; spider-sense **FIRST APPEARANCE:** *Amazing Spider-Man: Renew Your Vows* #2 (Feb 2017)

On Earth-18119, the wife of Peter Parker, Mary Jane Watson-Parker, is becoming increasingly concerned about the danger her husband and daughter's spider-powers place their family in. When Spider-Man is captured, Watson-Parker steals an armored suit from a minion of the villain who has taken her husband. Later, Peter Parker adapts the tech in the armor to build her a suit that replicates his own powers. Watson-Parker calls herself Spinneret and teams up with her husband against Super Villain the Mole Man. However, Spinneret's suit drains Spider-Man's powers when they are in close proximity to each other. To prevent him from becoming too weak, she swaps her armor for a Venom symbiote suit.

SCARLET SPIDER

REAL NAME: Benjamin Reilly **POWERS:** Super-strength, stamina, durability, agility, and reflexes; wall-crawling; spider-sense **FIRST APPEARANCE:** *Amazing Spider-Man* #149 (Oct 1975)

29 St

Ri

Scarlet Spider

When it comes to the radical science of cloning, no one has made more impact than crazed scientist Miles Warren and the various duplicates he has produced. The person whose DNA most frequently appears in Warren's petri dish is Spider-Man, whom Warren blames for the death of his beloved Gwen Stacy. Spider-Man clone Ben Reilly is one of the more successful products of Warren's lab. Carrying Peter Parker's DNA, Reilly is fundamentally too good-hearted to do Warren's evil bidding. After a difficult period of uncertain wandering, Reilly finds a niche as hero Scarlet Spider. However, his status as a clone means that Warren almost views him as a possession, at one point keeping him in a cruel cycle of death and rebirth in an attempt to iron out glitches with cellular degeneration.

KAINE

REAL NAME: Kaine **POWERS:** Super-strength, agility, and reflexes; wall-crawling; spider-sense; organic web production; burning touch **FIRST APPEARANCE:** *Web of Spider-Man* #119 (Dec 1994)

41 Vo

K

Kaine

Kaine is the result of scientist Miles Warren's first attempt at cloning Peter Parker. He is also a walking example of what can happen when experiments go wrong. Initially considered a success, a glitch during the cloning process causes Kaine's physical and mental state to deteriorate, and he nurses a searing hatred for his clone brother Ben Reilly. He is naturally more brutal than the original Spider-Man, but Kaine does find redemption by dying to save Spider-Man from Kraven the Hunter. He is born again, but Warren has tampered with his DNA to make him resemble a tarantula. Kaine is later cured of his condition, and his previous degeneration issues. He is then able to take up more of a heroic role than previously, even joining up with some superteams.

X-23

REAL NAME: Laura Kinney **POWERS:** Super-strength, stamina, durability, agility, reflexes, and senses; healing factor; bone claws in hands and feet **FIRST APPEARANCE:** *NYX* #3 (Feb 2004)

X-23 is a clone created as part of a top-secret program to produce another Wolverine. Since the only DNA sample the scientists possess has a damaged Y chromosome, they cannot produce an exact male copy of Logan, so they create a female clone instead. Mutant geneticist Sarah Kinney successfully makes an embryo using Wolverine DNA combined with her own, and gestates it in her own body. The child, who has two long claws that can pop from each wrist and one in each foot, is brought up to be a living weapon. Rarely treated with kindness, as she grows up she struggles with self-loathing. However, when she meets Logan and the X-Men, and takes her clone "father's" mantle of Wolverine, Kinney starts working toward a healthier mindset and a life of her own.

STRYFE

REAL NAME: Stryfe **POWERS:** Super-strength, speed, stamina, agility, and reflexes; psionic abilities, including telepathy and telekinesis **FIRST APPEARANCE:** *New Mutants* #87 (Mar 1990)

Stryfe is a clone of Nathan Summers, aka Cable, who is himself the son of the Jean Grey clone Madelyne Pryor and mutant Scott Summers (Cyclops). When time-traveler Cable is brought into the future to find a cure for his techno-organic virus, it is feared that he will not survive and so a clone is created that possesses all of Cable's psionic mutant abilities. As a child, this clone is taken by immortal mutant Apocalypse and intensely trained and genetically enhanced to make him worthy of one day becoming a host body for Apocalypse. However, Apocalypse mistakenly believes that Stryfe is actually Nathan Summers, and when he finds out that he is in fact a clone of him, his transference into Stryfe's body does not take place. Filled with hate, Stryfe ends up pursuing Cable through time.

DOCTOR OCTOPUS

7	Vo
Oo	
Doctor Octopus	

REAL NAME: Otto Octavius **POWERS:** Genius intelligence; mentally controlled metal tentacles **FIRST APPEARANCE:** *Amazing Spider-Man* #3 (Jul 1963)

Otto Octavius's genius for science leads him down some unexpected paths in life. While he also acquires additional abilities following a radiation accident and, later, after taking over Peter Parker's spider-powered body, it is the phenomenal intelligence he is born with that is Octavius's real "super-power." Octavius is working at a nuclear plant when he designs a set of metal tentacles that help him keep his distance while handling toxic materials. However, when he is caught in a radiation explosion, his tentacles suddenly adhere to his body, and he can control them with his mind. The radiation also causes brain damage, turning Octavius into a paranoid megalomaniac.

EGGHEAD

2	Vo
Eg	
Egghead	

REAL NAME: Elihas Starr **POWERS:** Genius intelligence; a rejuvenating serum that can bring him back to life **FIRST APPEARANCE:** *Tales to Astonish* #38 (Dec 1962)

It is a great shame that some people blessed with extraordinary intellects do not use them to advance humanity and instead only apply them to coming up with new ways of enriching themselves and putting others down. Elihas Starr, cruelly nicknamed Egghead on account of his appearance, is just such a man. A talented atomic scientist, Starr is sacked for espionage and decides to embark on a career in crime. Although he builds a variety of ingenious devices for his schemes, perhaps his greatest scientific achievement is the Rejuvetech serum that allows him to return to life after being killed by Avenger Hawkeye.

JACKAL

20	Vo
Jc	
Jackal	

REAL NAME: Miles Warren **POWERS:** Genius intelligence **FIRST APPEARANCE:** *Amazing Spider-Man* #129 (Feb 1974)

Miles Warren is originally a biochemist who later develops a specialized interest in cloning. Having already lost his family in a tragic accident caused by his scientific work, he becomes completely unstable after the death of one of his students, Gwen Stacy, for whom he has developed deep feelings. He takes the ethically dubious decision to begin attempting to clone human beings, with the aim of bringing Stacy back. When his lab partner questions him, Warren kills him, manifesting a split personality known as the Jackal to absolve himself of responsibility for his actions. As the Jackal, he wears a green costume but later creates a formula that actually turns his body into its Jackal form.

TINKERER

5	Vo
Tk	
Tinkerer	

REAL NAME: Phineas Mason **POWERS:** Genius intelligence, particularly with gadgets and weaponry **FIRST APPEARANCE:** *Amazing Spider-Man* #2 (May 1963)

As the Tinkerer, Phineas Mason uses his flair for constructing, repairing, and improving on innovative gadgets and weapons to make money as the go-to repairman for the Super-Villain community. He opts for this course after initially attempting to be a Super Villain himself. Under his alias of the Terrible Tinkerer, Mason has an early run-in with Spider-Man that shows him there is ultimately less risk to himself if he is not personally carrying out evil plans, but merely facilitating others. One of his most devious schemes is building a robot "brother," whom he names Hophni Mason and uses as a Trojan horse to gain the trust of Super Heroes and amass valuable intelligence about them.

MOLTEN MAN

14	Co
Rx	
Molten Man	

REAL NAME: Mark Raxton **POWERS:** Super-strength, stamina, and durability; heat generation; fiery blasts **FIRST APPEARANCE:** *Amazing Spider-Man* #28 (Sep 1965)

Mark Raxton is a scientist who works with robotics expert Dr. Spencer Smythe to develop a liquid metal alloy from material extracted from a meteor. Raxton becomes impatient to monetize his share of the alloy and steals the only sample, but he smashes the jar and spills the liquid over himself. His skin absorbs the substance and he becomes the Molten Man—his body as strong as metal but still flexible. As the effects of the alloy develop, Raxton's body becomes super-heated and begins giving off radiation, gradually killing him. Eventually a cure is found for his condition, and Raxton is able to begin making a new life for himself.

GRAVITON

31	Vo
Gn	
Graviton	

REAL NAME: Franklin Hall **POWERS:** Controls the gravity of objects with his mind **FIRST APPEARANCE:** *Avengers* #158 (Apr 1977)

Franklin Hall's specialty in the world of science is research into teleportation. When an experiment goes wrong, Hall absorbs subnuclear graviton particles and discovers that he can control gravity. His powers cause his fellow scientists to fear him, so Hall decides to use them to create his own personal fiefdom, isolating his whole research facility and making himself its overlord. His mental control over gravity means that he can make objects super-heavy or feather-light, and he can also cause objects to be attracted to one another and fuse together. His power is so great that he can even lift a whole city. He is later driven insane by a Cosmic Cube—a reality-warping object that can control energy and matter.

DEATHLOK

REAL NAME: Luther Manning **POWERS:** Super-strength, stamina, durability, agility, and reflexes; computer brain **FIRST APPEARANCE:** *Astonishing Tales* #25 (Aug 1974)

25   St

Dk

Deathlok

On Earth-7484, Colonel Luther Manning is killed. This is not the end for him, however, as Manning's corpse is selected for a top-secret program to create an army of super-powered cyborgs from deceased humans. He is born again as Deathlok, a perfect killing machine. Although the procedure is physically successful, Deathlok's creators had not planned on his human personality reasserting itself and embarking on an inner struggle with "Puter," his computerized programming. The glitches in Deathlok do not dissuade people across realities from building more cyborgs in the same manner, sometimes even using other versions of Manning to do it. The original travels the Multiverse searching for a purpose. Although he now has super-powers, Manning's dearest wish is simply to be human again.

LADY DEATHSTRIKE

REAL NAME: Yuriko Oyama **POWERS:** Super-strength, speed, durability, agility, and reflexes; healing factor; Adamantium nails **FIRST APPEARANCE:** *Uncanny X-Men* #205 (May 1986)

36   Vo

Ld

Lady
Deathstrike

Yuriko Oyama is Lady Deathstrike, an expert martial artist whose skills are not enough to achieve her ultimate goal—to extract Wolverine's Adamantium skeleton. This is too much for any normal human to achieve, so Deathstrike takes an extreme step: she volunteers to be transmutated into a cyborg. She emerges from the painful process a cybernetic organism—a living weapon. As well as enhanced strength and stamina, she has unbreakable claws like Wolverine, but in Deathstrike's case, there are 10—one extending from each fingernail. The procedure also grafts Adamantium onto her skeleton so that she can match Wolverine in durability. Deathstrike's willingness to give up her humanity in the single-minded pursuit of her target speaks volumes about her mindset.

KORVAC

REAL NAME: Michael Korvac **POWERS:** Almost limitless powers **FIRST APPEARANCE:** *Giant-Size Defenders* #3 (Jan 1975)

Michael Korvac is one of the most powerful cyborgs ever to have existed. In an alternate future timeline in which Earth is invaded by aliens the Brotherhood of the Badoon, Korvac has the lower half of his body replaced by a computer. Filled with resentment, Korvac later significantly increases his threat levels by siphoning off power first from Elder of the Universe the Grandmaster and then from the cosmic entity Galactus's worldship. Now possessing the almighty Power Cosmic, Korvac's megalomanaical tendencies are awoken, and the Multiverse is at the mercy of his pursuit of his twin obsessions: his love, Carina, and becoming a god. After apparently being killed, Korvac is resurrected as an android.

GUARDIAN

REAL NAME: James Hudson **POWERS:** Super-strength; supersonic flight; force-field creation; teleporting; blasts **FIRST APPEARANCE:** *Alpha Flight* #89 (Oct 1990)

James Hudson, a cybernetics expert and founder of the Canadian superteam Alpha Flight, wears a super-suit of his own design and fights as the hero Guardian.

When his suit explodes midbattle, Hudson is believed killed, but he is, in fact, thrust into the space-time continuum. He is rescued thousands of years into the past by the alien Qwrlln, who believe his damaged suit to be a part of him, and "rebuild" him accordingly as a cyborg. He is put into stasis until his own time, at which point his cyborg mind awakes. He returns to active duty with Alpha Flight, although his cyborg status means that he is not quite the same person he once was.

BETA RAY BILL

REAL NAME: Beta Ray Bill **POWERS:** Super-strength, speed, and stamina; healing factor; longevity; magical Stormbreaker weapon **FIRST APPEARANCE:** *Thor* #337 (Nov 1983)

Beta Ray Bill is the last hope of his race, the Korbinites, who choose him as their champion to seek out a new planetary home for them when theirs is destroyed. To increase Bill's strength, his people transform him into a cyborg. On his travels, Bill comes across Asgardian god Thor's enchanted hammer, Mjolnir, and gains Thor's power. Bill is then commanded by Thor's father, Odin, to fight Thor for the weapon. Bill wins the fight but does not take Mjolnir. Instead, Odin forges a new hammer for him—Stormbreaker—out of powerful uru metal. This cyborg is now one of the most fearsome warriors in the universe, but in true heroic fashion, Bill remains a noble being.

MISTY KNIGHT

REAL NAME: Mercedes "Misty" Knight **POWERS:** Bionic arm gives super-strength and viselike grip; martial arts and detective skills **FIRST APPEARANCE:** *Marvel Premiere* #21 (Mar 1975)

27 St

Kn

Misty Knight

Heroic NYPD officer Misty Knight is given a bionic arm by Tony Stark when she loses hers in a bomb blast in the line of duty. Since Misty is no longer considered able to be a street cop, she leaves to set up her own private investigation agency

with best friend Colleen Wing. Knight's bionic arm is the only part of her that is mechanical, but successive upgrades through the years grant her a range of capabilities. The first arm increases Knight's strength and gives her a viselike grip, but its replacement goes even further, being constructed of a Vibranium-diamond alloy and having a freeze-blast facility. Later upgrades give Knight the ability to emit concussive energy blasts and produce an energy shield. One upgrade even includes claws similar to those of Wolverine's.

NEBULA

REAL NAME: Nebula **POWERS:** Super-strength and durability; telescopic bionic arm with energy cannon; bionic eye with probability generator **FIRST APPEARANCE:** *Avengers* #257 (Jul 1985)

35 Vo

Ne

Nebula

Nebula, granddaughter of Titanian warlord Thanos, commits terrible deeds and even wields the immense power of the Infinity Stones, but when her past catches up with her, the trauma sends her into total neurological shutdown. She is taken to

criminal surgeon Dr. Mandibus, who restructures all her higher functions and gives her a bionic left arm and left eye. The arm is telescopic and also contains an energy cannon in the palm of the hand. The eye contains a probability-assessing capability, which vastly increases Nebula's tactical and strategic abilities. Later, Nebula spends time in the power source known as the God Quarry, which further augments her powers. She can exist in space without the need for a suit or life-support systems and hold her own against powerful beings like Asgardians.

VICTOR MANCHA

44   St

Vm

Victor Mancha

REAL NAME: Victor Mancha **POWERS:** Super-strength, stamina, and durability; electromagnetic powers; self-repair **FIRST APPEARANCE:** *Runaways* #1 (Apr 2005)

Victor Mancha is the result of a bizarre cooperation between the evil android Ultron and a former drugs mule, Marianella Mancha. Ultron plans to create a cyborg indistinguishable in appearance from a human, with the intention of one day using it to infiltrate and destroy the Avengers. He uses Mancha's DNA and combines it with a nanite skeleton to create a fully grown "teenager," implanted with memories of a childhood he never had so that even he does not know what he is. As time goes on, the nanites will morph into a substance exactly resembling human cells. However, when Mancha discovers the truth about his origins, he rejects Ultron and his plans.

KLAW

16   Vo

Kl

Klaw

REAL NAME: Ulysses Klaw **POWERS:** Super-strength, and speed; intangibility; invulnerability; sound manipulation **FIRST APPEARANCE:** *Fantastic Four* #53 (Aug 1966)

Ulysses Klaw is a physicist working with sound who discovers how to convert sound waves into a physical form. Requiring the near-indestructible metal Vibranium to take his research further, Klaw travels to the African region of Wakanda and tries to take the substance by force. In the violence that ensues, Klaw loses his hand. Later he uses his own technology to construct a prosthetic that features a scaled-down version of his sound-converter device. Klaw also uses his device on himself and becomes a being made from sound. In this form, he is almost invulnerable because his body can reform even if it is destroyed, although he has a weakness to Vibranium.

ANCILLARY EXEMPLARS

54   St

Ny

Nanny

53   St

Nu

Nuke

55   St

Os

Omega Sentinel

52   St

Uy

Spider-Slayer

Not all cyborgs closely resemble humans. **Nanny** is a mutant scientist imprisoned in an egg-shaped cyborg body of her own making.

She is obsessed with taking and protecting mutant children. Meanwhile, **Nuke** is created by the Weapon Plus program to be a humanlike cyborg with little remaining humanity. The **Omega Sentinel** is one of many humans implanted with Sentinel technology. And **Spider-Slayer** creates cybernetic enhancements for his body after being injured in battle with Spider-Man.

DOCTOR FAUSTUS

REAL NAME: Johann Fennhoff **POWERS:** Genius intellect, especially in psychology and psychiatry; powers of persuasion **FIRST APPEARANCE:** *Captain America* #107 (Nov 1968)

21	Vo
Fa	
Doctor Faustus	

It could be said that the most dangerous field of science is psychology. A person who has studied the human mind and knows how to bend it to their own will possesses enormous power, and if that individual has evil intentions, they are an opponent to be feared. Doctor Faustus is just such an individual. He is one of the world's foremost psychiatrists, but he is also an expert in hypnosis—one with no ethical qualms about using his patients as pawns for his own selfish ends.

Faustus is very proud of his voice, believing it to be one of the most important tools of his trade. He can alter its modulation to either be highly persuasive to the listener or to deliver a jarring shock. Although he is physically large, Doctor Faustus does not have super-strength or durability. On some occasions, when his corrupt plans have led to fierce run-ins with Super Heroes, he has become badly injured and, as a result, is often seen using walking aids or relying on a wheelchair.

TOOLS OF THE TRADE

As well as his own skills, Doctor Faustus uses an array of hallucinogenics and other drugs to disorient his victims and render them as suggestible as possible. He then forces them to relive the traumatic moments of their pasts, ostensibly to cure them of their mental troubles, but in reality to plunge them into a state of fear so that they can be brainwashed or just broken according to his whim. To help him make his victims' traumatic visions as vivid as possible, sometimes Faustus employs henchmen as actors and uses props to recreate scenes from their lives. He is a true master of manipulation.

Although he is physically imposing, Doctor Faustus's prime asset is his brain. His knowledge of it coupled with his lack of ethics make him a dangerous villain.

MAD THINKER

REAL NAME: Unknown **POWERS:** Genius intelligence, especially in robotics and computer science; eidetic memory **FIRST APPEARANCE:** *Fantastic Four* #15 (Jun 1963)

6	Vo
Te	
Mad Thinker	

The Mad Thinker specializes in the science of probabilities. He uses his genius for computing and engineering to build devices that predict the likely outcomes of different scenarios, then applies this knowledge for criminal gain.

Perhaps one of his cleverest gadgets is the implant in his head that enables him to remotely control his androids and monitor what is going on his labs, as this means he can continue his work even while incarcerated. Although he is a phenomenally intelligent person, the Mad Thinker lacks imagination, and this prevents him from being a truly great inventor. Many of his more successful android creations are based on the work of others. He is also often thwarted by the unpredictability of his opponents, which is not foreseen by his machines.

MOONDRAGON

REAL NAME: Heather Douglas **POWERS:** Enhanced strength, stamina, durability; extremely powerful psionic abilities; martial arts skills **FIRST APPEARANCE:** *Iron Man* #54 (Jan 1973)

23	St
Do	
Moondragon	

When her family is killed by Thanos, Earth girl Heather Douglas is taken under the wing of the Titanian Eternal's father and brought up in a religious community on his homeworld of Titan. Here, she learns how to realize her huge psionic potential and names herself Moondragon, after apparently resisting the influence of the powerful entity called the Dragon of the Moon. Her telepathic abilities are almost second to none, and certainly among the most powerful ever manifested by an Earthling. She is not a mutant, whose power is part of her genetic makeup, but owes her abilities to her extraordinary levels of concentration, honed while studying with Titan's monks. While there, Douglas also learns martial arts and how to use her concentration to increase her strength and durability levels.

HAWKEYE (CLINT BARTON)

REAL NAME: Clint Barton **POWERS:** Peak-human strength, durability, and reflexes; master marksman; martial arts; weapons design **FIRST APPEARANCE:** *Tales of Suspense* #57 (Sep 1964)

10	St
Hw	
Hawkeye (Clint Barton)	

Clint Barton is the epitome of a naturally skilled peak human. With no super-powers, healing factor, or armor, he lines up alongside Earth's Mightiest Heroes and is an accepted and long-standing member of a superteam that has included gods. Barton's best-known attribute is his outstanding talent with a bow and arrows. Although his marksmanship is a natural gift, Barton must also train for as many hours as he can, for he knows that, as a nonpowered Avenger, he cannot afford to miss. Barton is also an ingenious designer of a vast range of trick arrows. These clever weapons, with various applications for particular mission situations—such as explosives, gas-releasing projectiles, and cables for swinging on—give Hawkeye an extra edge when he is facing villains many times more powerful than him.

HAWKEYE (KATE BISHOP)

REAL NAME: Kate Bishop **POWERS:** Master marksman; martial arts and swordsmanship skills; peak-human athleticism **FIRST APPEARANCE:** *Young Avengers* #1 (Apr 2005)

43	St
Kb	
Hawkeye (Kate Bishop)	

Brought up as a wealthy socialite, Kate Bishop is anything but a spoiled little rich girl. She has a natural sense of justice and a desire to spend her life helping others. She is a fan of the Avengers, but especially Hawkeye, whom she admires for fighting Super Villains with just his own skill. Taking lessons in fencing and archery, Bishop discovers that she is just as naturally skilled with a bow as her hero. Later, she joins the Young Avengers and is officially given the code name Hawkeye while Clint Barton is missing. When Barton eventually returns, Bishop keeps the name with his blessing, and they become friends and partners in fighting crime. However, Bishop also chooses to spend time separately from Barton so that she can forge her own identity as Hawkeye.

KINGPIN

REAL NAME: Wilson Fisk **POWERS:** Peak-human strength and durability; skilled martial artist **FIRST APPEARANCE:** *Amazing Spider-Man* #50 (Jul 1967)

Wilson Fisk is the Kingpin, ruler of New York City's underworld. Although he might choose to let his underlings handle most of his dirty work, the Kingpin is more than capable of taking on the physical side of business when he needs to. His strength is comparable to an Olympic-level weight lifter, and his intimidating physical bulk is almost entirely made up of muscle. He trains himself in martial arts and in the traditional Japanese sport of sumo wrestling. Kingpin is the archetypal self-made man, having pulled himself up from a poverty-stricken background to be an influential, educated person, albeit one whose formidable talents are turned to organized crime.

PUNISHER

REAL NAME: Frank Castle **POWERS:** Peak-human strength, stamina, agility, and reflexes; martial arts **FIRST APPEARANCE:** *Amazing Spider-Man* #129 (Feb 1974)

Former Marine Frank Castle is on a one-man mission to bring down organized crime. His all-consuming crusade begins when his family is murdered by gangsters.

As the Punisher, Castle has no super-powers to call upon—just his extensive military and special-forces training, expertise with an array of weapons, and an unshakable desire for brutal justice. While his cause may be just, his methods are well outside the acceptable parameters for most Super Heroes. Villains know that if they are caught by regular heroes, they can expect to end up in jail, but if they fall into the hands of the Punisher, the outlook is far more bleak.

BULLSEYE

REAL NAME: Lester **POWERS:** Master marksman and assassin; highly skilled martial artist; Adamantium-enhanced bones **FIRST APPEARANCE:** *Daredevil* #131 (Mar 1976)

He is one of the world's most deadly assassins, but little is known about how Bullseye came to acquire his lethal skillset. Information about his past tends to come via Bullseye himself, and he covers his tracks with misrepresentations of the facts. Bullseye's sanity is often called into question, adding another layer of unpredictability to his behavior. What is known about Bullseye is that he is almost unmatched in his ability to find a target. He is also adept at using unusual objects as weapons. Although for the first part of his career as a killer-for-hire Bullseye relies solely on his natural talent, after a near-fatal run-in with Daredevil, he is given Adamantium upgrades to his bones, making him far more durable.

MOON KNIGHT

REAL NAME: Marc Spector **POWERS:** Extensive military training; armored suit; crescent-shaped throwing blades **FIRST APPEARANCE:** *Werewolf by Night* #32 (Aug 1975)

Moon Knight, aka Marc Spector, is one of the most enigmatic Super Heroes there is. Born a human with no powers, as an adult he acquires abilities linked to the phases of the moon, said to be derived from the Egyptian god Khonshu. As the god's avatar, Moon Knight protects those who travel by night. Spector suffers from dissociative personality disorder and, in the past, questioned whether Khonshu was another of his personalities, but Khonshu was ultimately proven to be a separate deity. Khonshu will occasionally bestow temporary powers on Spector, though it is uncertain whether Spector's mental illness is so acute that he imagined these into being. Spector possesses huge personal wealth, which he uses to fund his crime-fighting endeavors with a high-tech suit and an impressive array of weapons.

KA-ZAR

REAL NAME: Kevin Plunder **POWERS:** Peak-human strength, speed, stamina, durability, agility, and reflexes; highly skilled hunter **FIRST APPEARANCE:** *X-Men* #10 (Mar 1965)

Kevin Plunder is a British aristocrat by birth, but fate separates him from his family and brings him to the Savage Land, a hidden jungle in Antarctica. He becomes the protector of this strange land-out-of-time, nurtured as he grows from a boy to a man by a saber-toothed tiger named Zabu. The Savage Land needs protection, not only because of the presumed-extinct species that still flourish there but also because it is a source of a particular strain of the rare energy-manipulating metal Vibranium. Ka-Zar, as Plunder becomes known, is later joined in his mission by Shanna, who becomes his wife. Both are later given superhuman abilities and a mystical connection to the living things of their realm when they are immersed in vapors imbued with the spirit of the Savage Land.

CROSSBONES

37   Vo
Rw
Crossbones

REAL NAME: Brock Rumlow **POWERS:** Peak-human strength, speed, and reflexes; martial arts; marksmanship **FIRST APPEARANCE:** *Captain America* #359 (Oct 1989)

Brock Rumlow is a highly trained mercenary and assassin. Handpicked by the Red Skull to be one of his special operatives, he is given the code name Crossbones. Although Crossbones has shown glimmers of potential rehabilitation, he ultimately always returns to the Hydra organization's cause and the Red Skull. It seems likely that Rumlow's actions, usually evidencing too much hate and not enough empathy, are informed by a mental condition like psychopathy, which goes back to his childhood. Despite possessing no permanent super-powers, Crossbones still manages to be one of Captain America's deadliest opponents.

MYSTERIO

8   Vo
Qb
Mysterio

REAL NAME: Quentin Beck **POWERS:** Special effects and robotics expert; genius inventor **FIRST APPEARANCE:** *Amazing Spider-Man* #13 (Jun 1964)

Although he looks like an alien or wielder of dark magic, Mysterio is a regular human with no super-powers. Despite this, he has managed to become one of Spider-Man's longest-standing foes. Quentin Beck is a fan of movies and uses his genius for engineering and invention to forge a career in special effects. However, he decides to shoot for greater fame by becoming the person who defeats Spider-Man. He applies his talents for illusion to become Mysterio, a costumed criminal whose one-way glass helmet gives him an unsettling appearance. His suit is equipped with gadgets that enable him to project holograms or release hallucinogens to disorient even the strongest of opponents.

ANCILLARY EXEMPLARS

51   St
Sv
Silver Sable

50   Vo
Bo
Boomerang

56   Vo
Ly
Lady Bullseye

49   Vo
Bc
Batroc

Silver Sable is a hunter of war criminals whose willpower and fighting skills make up for her lack of super-powers. **Boomerang** uses his incredible pitching ability and flair for designing weaponized boomerangs to forge his criminal career. **Lady Bullseye** is inspired by her male namesake to become a skilled assassin, training to the highest level in various forms of hand-to-hand combat. And **Batroc** uses his expertise in savate, a French martial art, and talent for leaping to become a thief and mercenary.

S.H.I.E.L.D.

FIRST APPEARANCE: *Strange Tales* #135 (Aug 1965)

13	Ba

Ie
S.H.I.E.L.D.

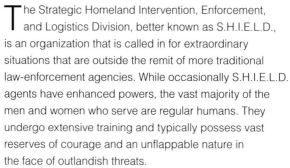

The Strategic Homeland Intervention, Enforcement, and Logistics Division, better known as S.H.I.E.L.D., is an organization that is called in for extraordinary situations that are outside the remit of more traditional law-enforcement agencies. While occasionally S.H.I.E.L.D. agents have enhanced powers, the vast majority of the men and women who serve are regular humans. They undergo extensive training and typically possess vast reserves of courage and an unflappable nature in the face of outlandish threats.

S.H.I.E.L.D. is the brainchild of businessman Howard Stark, who sees the need for a secret organization to combat terrorism, especially the subversive forces of Hydra. His idea is taken to the US government and then endorsed by the United Nations. The first director of S.H.I.E.L.D. is Rick Stoner, but when he is killed, the Executive Council invites Nick Fury to step into the vacancy. Fury surrounds himself with a handpicked team of trusted comrades, including his right-hand man from his army days, Thaddeus "Dum Dum" Dugan. Other key agents at that time include Clay Quartermain and European aristocrat Valentina de la Fontaine.

Sharon Carter, aka Agent 13, is one of S.H.I.E.L.D.'s top people for many years. It is a legacy that runs in her family, as her aunt, Peggy Carter, is also a S.H.I.E.L.D. agent. The elder Carter is well used to putting herself at risk for a noble cause, having spent World War II undertaking extermely dangerous missions for the French Resistance.

When Fury is removed from his position as director, he is replaced by one of the new generation of S.H.I.E.L.D. agents, Maria Hill. She is then succeeded by Daisy

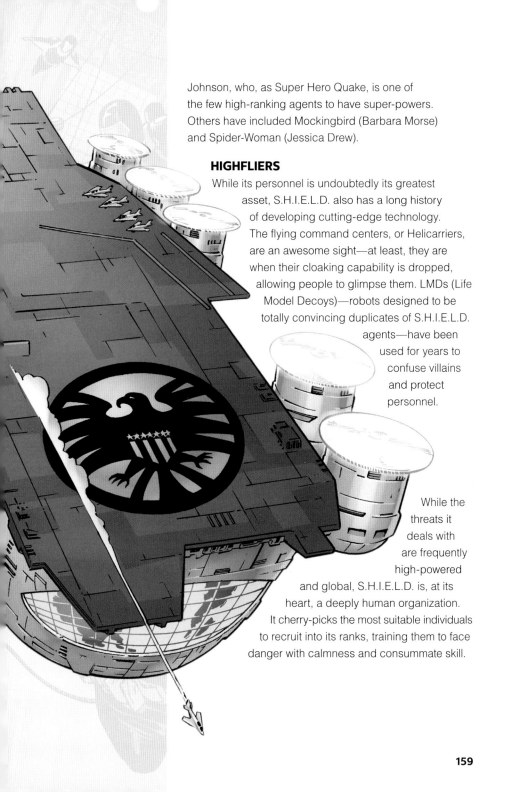

Johnson, who, as Super Hero Quake, is one of the few high-ranking agents to have super-powers. Others have included Mockingbird (Barbara Morse) and Spider-Woman (Jessica Drew).

HIGHFLIERS

While its personnel is undoubtedly its greatest asset, S.H.I.E.L.D. also has a long history of developing cutting-edge technology. The flying command centers, or Helicarriers, are an awesome sight—at least, they are when their cloaking capability is dropped, allowing people to glimpse them. LMDs (Life Model Decoys)—robots designed to be totally convincing duplicates of S.H.I.E.L.D. agents—have been used for years to confuse villains and protect personnel.

While the threats it deals with are frequently high-powered and global, S.H.I.E.L.D. is, at its heart, a deeply human organization. It cherry-picks the most suitable individuals to recruit into its ranks, training them to face danger with calmness and consummate skill.

EXTRADIMENSIONAL FORCES

Often the most formidable individuals draw their powers from other dimensions. Some beings are personifications of concepts so far beyond human understanding that the very fact of their existence is hard to accept.

Gd GODS

What humans see as gods—the mighty Asgardians and Olympians— are actually powerful beings visiting Earth from other dimensions.

4 St	6 St	5 Vo	42 St	20 Vo	7 St	14 St
Th	**O**	**L**	**Tj**	**Hs**	**Hi**	**Ls**
Thor	Odin	Loki	Thor (Jane Foster)	Hercules	Heimdall	Sif

13 Vo	45 St	65 St	44 St	48 St	39 Vo	18 Vo
Qd	**Fi**	**Ka**	**Bd**	**Wt**	**Ev**	**Fg**
Hela	Frigga	Karnilla	Balder	Warriors Three	Malekith	Frost Giants

28 Ba	22 Vo	16 Vo	15 Vo
Vk	**A**	**Ex**	**En**
Valkyrie	Ares	Executioner	Enchantress

Ab ABSTRACT BEINGS

The vastness of the Multiverse demands that somewhere there must be all-powerful forces that created it and watch over it still.

40 St	21 St	24 St	1 St
Jk	**Et**	**Lt**	**Dt**
One-Above-All	Eternity	Living Tribunal	Death

36 St	57 St	46 St	53 St	58 St	60 St	52 St
Cx	**By**	**Ts**	**Pf**	**Ob**	**Ey**	**Eo**
Chaos and Order	Beyonder	Stranger	Phoenix Force	Oblivion	Entropy	Eon

GOD-GIVEN

The Black Panther—one of Earth's most impressive heroes—is not a god himself, but he does derive a significant portion of his power from a divine source.

23	St
Bp	
Black Panther	

MYSTICAL

The world of magic and mysticism encompasses heroes and villains who often battle in existential struggles that happen out of sight of regular mortals.

8	St
Dc	
Doctor Strange	

12	St	3	Vo	30	St
Wh		**Vd**		**Vo**	
Scarlet Witch		Doctor Doom		Doctor Voodoo	

35	St	9	St	41	St
B		**On**		**Wc**	
Captain Britain		The Ancient One		Wiccan	

49	St	43	St	54	St
Ag		**Du**		**Bl**	
Agatha Harkness		Doctor Druid		Black Cat	

50	Vo	64	St	47	Co
Tg		**Ac**		**Dy**	
Tigra		America Chavez		Destroyer	

DEMONIC

Powers gained through a demonic source are often hard to resist, but the demons who bestow them always make sure they get something in return.

17	Co
Du	
Dormammu	

11	Vo	10	Vo	27	Co
Bn		**Ng**		**Gr**	
Baron Mordo		Nightmare		Ghost Rider	

25	St	26	Co	31	St
Dw		**Li**		**Dl**	
Black Knight		Mephisto		Hellstrom	

55	Vo	59	Vo	56	St	29	St	2	Vo	37	Vo	19	Vo
Ek		**Pk**		**G**		**Eb**		**Vl**		**Hn**		**Ju**	
Elektra		The Hood		Gargoyle		Blade		Dracula		The Hand		Juggernaut	

CHI

The life force of chi runs through all living beings, but only a select few have learned how to channel it to gain superhuman abilities.

33	St
If	
Iron Fist	

38	St	32	St	34	Vo	52	Vo	61	St	62	St	63	St
Sz		**Kf**		**Cw**		**Dv**		**Td**		**Po**		**Pm**	
Stick		Shang-Chi		Colleen Wing		Steel Serpent		Tiger's Beautiful Daughter		Prince of Orphans		Power Man	

THOR

REAL NAME: Thor Odinson **POWERS:** Longevity; super-senses; healing factor; flight; commands lightning; access to Thorforce **FIRST APPEARANCE:** *Journey into Mystery* #83 (Aug 1962)

There are some races in the Multiverse that are so far beyond humans in their strength and longevity that when they come into contact with Earthlings, they are worshipped as gods. This does not mean that their powers are in fact divine, only that Earth knowledge is not yet advanced enough to know the science behind them.

The Asgardians are not strictly speaking gods, but they are extremely powerful beings from a pocket dimension called Asgard. They possess phenomenal strength and endurance, living such long lives that to humans they can appear to be immortal. While they generally have abilities that set them far above humankind, Thor is exceptional even for an Asgardian. His father is Odin, King of Asgard, but his purported mother is Gaea, one of the Elder Gods. Thor's unique mixed heritage has made him stronger and more durable than other Asgardians.

As well as his physical attributes, Thor also possesses powers that are more mystical in nature. He inherits from his father, Odin, a force that enables him to become almost invincible for a period of time. However, excessive use of this "Thorforce" also weakens him and requires that he take a long sleep to recuperate his strength. While in the Thorsleep, Thor is vulnerable.

HAMMER OF THE GOD

Thor's key power is his command of storms, which justifiably earns him the sobriquet "God of Thunder." He can summon lightning and refocus its electrical energy as a powerful blast. He often uses this ability while wielding the hammer called Mjolnir. This hammer is forged for Thor by Odin, using super-strong uru metal. Mjolnir has

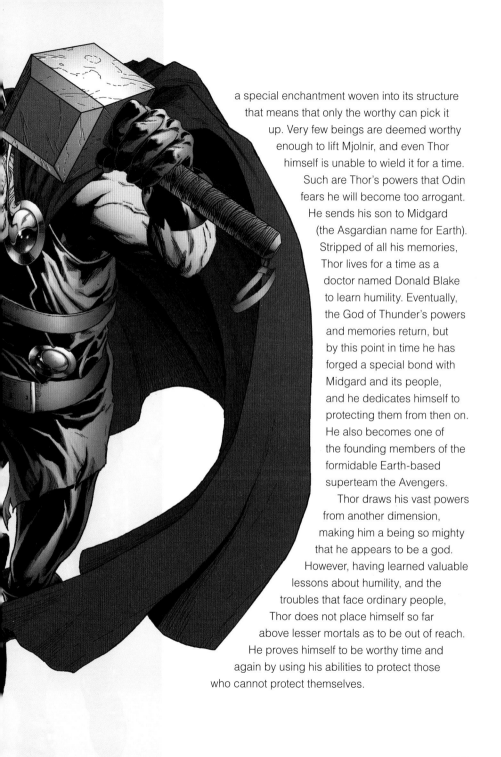

a special enchantment woven into its structure that means that only the worthy can pick it up. Very few beings are deemed worthy enough to lift Mjolnir, and even Thor himself is unable to wield it for a time. Such are Thor's powers that Odin fears he will become too arrogant. He sends his son to Midgard (the Asgardian name for Earth). Stripped of all his memories, Thor lives for a time as a doctor named Donald Blake to learn humility. Eventually, the God of Thunder's powers and memories return, but by this point in time he has forged a special bond with Midgard and its people, and he dedicates himself to protecting them from then on. He also becomes one of the founding members of the formidable Earth-based superteam the Avengers.

Thor draws his vast powers from another dimension, making him a being so mighty that he appears to be a god. However, having learned valuable lessons about humility, and the troubles that face ordinary people, Thor does not place himself so far above lesser mortals as to be out of reach. He proves himself to be worthy time and again by using his abilities to protect those who cannot protect themselves.

ODIN

REAL NAME: Odin Borson **POWERS:** Super-strength, speed, stamina, and agility; longevity; healing factor; energy powers; wisdom **FIRST APPEARANCE:** *Journey into Mystery* #85 (Oct 1962)

Odin is the All-Father of the Asgardians, making him the ruler of this godlike race. He is unusually strong, even for an Asgardian, and can harness the Odinforce to make himself even more powerful. However, if he uses this mystic power too much, he is forced to enter the Odinsleep to renew himself. Odin has been visiting Midgard (Earth) for millennia, and his awesome powers cause the inhabitants of this realm to worship him as king of the gods. He possesses great wisdom and knowledge, which he uses to rule well and also to guide his son Thor to become his worthy successor. Eventually, Odin deems Thor ready to take over his title of All-Father. Odin also wields numerous mystical weapons, principally the spear Gungnir, through which he channels his considerable energy powers.

LOKI

REAL NAME: Loki Laufeyson **POWERS:** Super-strength and speed; longevity; sorcery, including shape-shifting; genius intellect **FIRST APPEARANCE:** *Journey into Mystery* #85 (Oct 1962)

Loki is not like other Asgardians. By birth, he is actually one of the Frost Giants of Jotunheim. Yet he is not like other Frost Giants either, having been born much smaller than average. Loki is adopted by Odin the All-Father after he slays Loki's real father, Laufey, in battle. Raised in Asgard, Loki shares many of the same abilities as Asgardians, but he is also a master of sorcery. He can use magic to further augment his powers, to shape-shift, and to create illusions, among other abilities. His proficiency in deception earns him the title "God of Mischief," but Loki frequently crosses the line from mere mischief into something far darker. His trickery is often focused on trying to usurp his adopted brother Thor, whom Loki deeply resents for being the heir apparent in Asgard.

THOR (JANE FOSTER)

REAL NAME: Jane Foster **POWERS:** Super-strength, speed, stamina, agility, and reflexes; longevity; healing factor; commands lightning **FIRST APPEARANCE:** *Thor: God of Thunder* #25 (Nov 2014)

After the hammer Mjolnir is lost by Thor Odinson, it calls to Jane Foster to be its next wielder. She is suffering from cancer, but when Foster picks up the magical weapon, she is healthy again and inherits all the incredible powers that Thor once had. Foster takes on the identity of Thor and enters a new lease of life as a Super Hero. However, it is soon clear that, although she is healthy while transformed into Thor, as soon as she turns back into her normal self, she becomes sick again. And worse, the magic that turns her into Thor also wipes out any progress from her cancer treatment. Foster sacrifices her life to defeat the Asgardians' vengeful enemy Mangog, but Odin and Thor revive her. She gives up Mjolnir so that she can focus on getting well and later inherits the powers of the Asgardian Valkyrie.

HERCULES

REAL NAME: Hercules **POWERS:** Super-strength, speed, stamina, durability, agility, and reflexes; healing factor; immortality **FIRST APPEARANCE:** *Journey into Mystery Annual* #1 (Oct 1965)

Son of Zeus and the mortal Alcmene, Hercules is born a demigod. He is also breastfed by his Olympian stepmother Hera, which bestows further divine power onto him. Hercules is not Asgardian, but Olympian, and while the two share many abilities, Olympians are genuinely immortal rather than just very long-lived. Hercules grows to be stronger than any other Olympian. The Olympians live in a pocket dimension accessed from Earth via a portal on Mount Olympus in Greece. This proximity to Earth leads to the Ancient Greeks worshipping them as true gods. The Olympians are quick to anger and often fall out with each other. At one point, Zeus banishes the headstrong Hercules from Olympus, but he finds a new home with the Avengers, becoming an extremely heavy-hitting addition to the team.

HEIMDALL

REAL NAME: Heimdall **POWERS:** Super-strength, speed, stamina, agility, reflexes, and senses; longevity; healing factor **FIRST APPEARANCE:** *Journey into Mystery* #85 (Oct 1962)

Heimdall is a mighty warrior of Asgard, but he also has senses that are enhanced far beyond the usual Asgardian level. He can see, hear, and even smell over great distances and across the boundaries of the Nine Realms. It is these incredible abilities, combined with his prowess in battle, that lead him to be appointed by Odin as the guardian of the Bifrost—the mystical bridge linking Asgard and Midgard. Due to his heightened sensory perception, Heimdall has the ability to tune out extraneous information he picks up; otherwise, he would be overwhelmed and driven mad. He also uses his senses to detect the location of other Asgardians no matter where they are. At one point, Heimdall is blinded by the vengeful Mangog, but his sight later returns thanks to his healing factor.

SIF

REAL NAME: Sif **POWERS:** Super-strength, speed, stamina, durability, agility, and reflexes; longevity; healing factor **FIRST APPEARANCE:** *Journey into Mystery* #102 (Mar 1964)

Sif is an Asgardian warrior who exhibits all the typical attributes of an Asgardian, including advanced longevity and super-strength. One of the very best female combatants in Asgard, she wields an enchanted sword bequeathed her by Odin. The sword can also open portals between dimensions. As a child, Sif has distinctive golden hair, but pernicious Loki cuts it all off as part of a cruel prank. Sif's hair is grown back by dwarves, who use the dark of night to create it, so from then on, she has black hair. Although Sif and Thor are very close and even intend to marry, Sif loves Asgard too much to make a long-term home on Earth as Thor has done. Sif later takes over from her brother, Heimdall, as the guardian of the Bifrost—the so-called "Rainbow Bridge" that links Asgard and Midgard.

HELA

REAL NAME: Hela **POWERS:** Super-strength; healing factor; immortality; energy manipulation; control over life and death **FIRST APPEARANCE:** *Journey into Mystery* #102 (Mar 1964)

Hela's origin is shrouded in mystery. She possesses similar attributes to the Asgardians, but she is prophesied to be a great danger to that race. To try and mitigate against this threat, the Asgardian All-Father Odin confines Hela to the realm of the dead, where she becomes greedy to collect more souls. Half of Hela's body is dead and decaying, but she is in possession of a magical cloak that renders her completely healthy as long as she is touching it. Hela has control over life and death—a capability that makes her one of the most powerful Asgardians in existence. It also means that, unlike other Asgardians, Hela is truly immortal. She can also deploy magic to create astral projections of herself, which have the same powers as Hela would in person.

ANCILLARY EXEMPLARS

There are many Asgardians who share the strengths common to that race, but they often enjoy additional powers, too. As Odin's bride, **Frigga** is Queen of Asgard. She is a great warrior but also has a talent for sorcery. Even more powerful in the sphere of magic is **Karnilla**, the Norn Queen and coruler of Hel. Although she does not always seem to act in Asgard's best interests, her love for **Balder** softens her. Balder is one of Frigga's sons with Odin and half brother to Thor. He is known as the "God of Light," as he can produce an intense light beam to use as a weapon, and also as "Balder the Brave" for his unflagging courage in battle. Balder's destiny is inextricably linked with Ragnarok, as his death is prophesied to be the trigger for the coming of Ragnarok and the ensuing world-ending event. The **Warriors Three** are a group of Asgardians who are longtime allies of Thor. They are Volstagg, Hogun, and Fandral, nicknamed respectively the Voluminous, the Grim, and the Dashing.

MALEKITH

39	Vo
Ev	
Malekith	

REAL NAME: Malekith **POWERS:** Super-strength, speed, stamina, durability, and reflexes; immortality; healing factor; sorcery **FIRST APPEARANCE:** *Thor* #344 (Jun 1984)

Malekith comes from Svartalfheim, one of the Nine Realms. He is a Dark Elf— a race that possesses similar attributes to Asgardians in that they are far stronger and more durable than Midgard's humans. Some Dark Elves have an aptitude for wielding magic, and Malekith is one of these. He can shape-shift, even into a mistlike substance that travels through the air. He can also teleport and cross dimensions. Malekith suffers a brutal upbringing, spending his formative years clearing Dark Elf corpses from battlefields. He is then taken in as an apprentice to a wizard but ultimately kills his mentor, whose last act is to place a dark mark on Malekith's face to make his true murderous nature clear to all.

FROST GIANTS

18	Vo
Fg	
Frost Giants	

POWERS: Super-strength and durability; longevity; huge size **FIRST APPEARANCE:** *Journey into Mystery* #112 (Jan 1965)

Frost Giants come from the realm known as Jotunheim, where they prefer to inhabit the coldest regions. They are much larger than the inhabitants of the other realms, including Asgard and Midgard, and they have a different physical composition. A typical Frost Giant's muscles are 34 percent frozen water. Frost Giants have blue skin and a very thick skull that leaves little room for a brain. They reach heights in excess of 30 feet (9 meters), although Loki, adopted as an Asgardian, is a notable exception to both these traits. Extremely high temperatures cause Frost Giants to reduce in size, but they can be restored if exposed to the cold again.

VALKYRIE

28	Ba
Vk	
Valkyrie	

REAL NAME: Brunnhilde **POWERS:** Super-strength and stamina; longevity; healing factor; near-death perception **FIRST APPEARANCE:** *Defenders* #4 (Feb 1973)

Brunnhilde is an Asgardian chosen by the All-Father, Odin, to escort the souls of the honored dead to Valhalla. As the Valkyrie, she leads the warrior goddesses known as the Valkyrior, and she has a mystical sense that enables her to see when someone is near death. She can also teleport herself and another person or soul to the realm of the dead. Trapped by fellow Asgardian the Enchantress, Brunnhilde's mind ends up in the body of an Earth woman, and for a time, she fights alongside the Defenders superteam. She is a renowned warrior, most notably with a sword, and often rides a winged horse named Aragorn. When she is killed by Malekith, her spirit calls upon the human Jane Foster to be the next Valkyrie.

ARES

22	Vo
A	
Ares	

REAL NAME: Ares **POWERS:** Super-strength, durability, agility, and reflexes; immortality; healing factor; power to create wars **FIRST APPEARANCE:** *Thor* #129 (Jun 1966)

Ares is an Olympian—a super-strong being from the pocket dimension of Olympus. Worshipped by the ancients as the God of War, Ares can manipulate people to start conflict on a local up to a global scale. Not surprisingly, he is also a fearsome warrior himself, comfortable with almost any weapon imaginable. He wears battle armor and a distinctive crested helmet in the style of the Ancient Greek hoplite soldiers. Ares is the strongest of all the Olympians with the exception of Zeus and Hercules. Although often viewed as a malign influence on Earth, Ares has nevertheless sometimes fought alongside its Super Heroes. However, as an Olympian, he is hard to control and is not naturally a team player.

EXECUTIONER

16	Vo
Ex	
Executioner	

REAL NAME: Skurge **POWERS:** Super-strength; healing factor; fearsome warrior with enchanted Bloodaxe **FIRST APPEARANCE:** *Journey into Mystery* #103 (Apr 1964)

Skurge is half-Asgardian and half-Storm Giant, giving him physical attributes that differ slightly from regular Asgardians. Like Frost Giants, Storm Giants are from Jotunheim, but they live in the warmer regions of the realm. Surge's mixed heritage gives him even greater strength and stamina than most Asgardians, as well as unusually dense body tissue. He is often seen as an ally to the Enchantress, being so enraptured by her that he will do anything she commands. Although he is part of many nefarious plots over the years, Skurge dies a hero, defending a bridge against an army from Hel. His spirit goes to the afterlife in Valhalla.

ENCHANTRESS

15	Vo
En	
Enchantress	

REAL NAME: Amora **POWERS:** Longevity; healing factor; sorcery—making others fall in love with her **FIRST APPEARANCE:** *Journey into Mystery* #103 (Apr 1964)

Amora is an Asgardian with all the godlike attributes of that race, but she is best known for her mastery of magic. She is apprenticed when young to Karnilla, the Norn Queen. She learns a wide range of mystic arts, though she is ultimately sent away for her lack of discipline. Furthering her education by using her seduction skills to get close to other sorcerers, Amora grows into one of the more dangerous Asgardians. Her mastery of sorcery includes astral projections, telepathy, teleportation, the transmutation of objects with a kiss, and her tears turn into gold and diamonds. The Enchantress spends a lot of time on Midgard and frequently conspires against Thor, usually in league with someone else.

ONE-ABOVE-ALL

40	St
Jk	
One-Above-All	

REAL NAME: None **POWERS:** Omnipotence, omniscience, and omnipresence; creator of the Multiverse
FIRST APPEARANCE: *Fantastic Four* #511 (May 2004)

The concept of an abstract being is difficult for the human brain to comprehend. The very top of the tree as far as abstract—or any other—beings are concerned is the One-Above-All. Sometimes also known as the Above-All-Others, this abstract entity is thought to be responsible for the creation of the Multiverse. It possesses limitless power and knowledge and is omnipresent throughout all known realities. The One-Above-All is the only being to whom the cosmic entity the Living Tribunal is answerable. Although the One-Above-All's powers are immeasurable, a future version of the Titan Thanos is able to temporarily absorb it using a powerful artifact called an Astral Regulator.

ETERNITY

21	St
Et	
Eternity	

REAL NAME: Eternity **POWERS:** Virtually omnipotent; manipulation of space, time, or any form of matter
FIRST APPEARANCE: *Strange Tales* #138 (Nov 1965)

Eternity is an abstract being who represents the entire reality of Earth-616, including every consciousness within it. It exists everywhere in its reality simultaneously. Other realities all have their own versions of Eternity, and all of these stem from another, Multiversal Eternity. Earth-616's Eternity forms a "two-in-one" with its sister-self, Infinity, who represents the entirety of space within the universe. Eternity is usually only seen as a visible entity when the universe is under threat. Although Eternity dies with the universe, when the universe is reborn, so is Eternity, although paradoxically it also triggers the new universe's creation.

LIVING TRIBUNAL

24	St
Lt	
Living Tribunal	

REAL NAME: Living Tribunal **POWERS:** Near omnipotence; can cancel the powers of the Infinity Stones
FIRST APPEARANCE: *Strange Tales* #158 (Jul 1967)

The Living Tribunal is an immensely powerful cosmic entity whose purpose is to keep watch and take actions to maintain balance throughout the Multiverse. It is created by the One-Above-All, who is the only being superior to the Living Tribunal. The Tribunal manifests as a golden being with a three-faced head. One face is entirely hooded and represents necessity, one is partially hooded and represents revenge, and the third, unhooded face is for equity. All three faces must reach agreement before the Living Tribunal can pronounce a verdict in a case. Should such a judgment be reached, the Living Tribunal has both the authority and the physical power to destroy an inhabited planet.

DEATH

1   St
Dt
Death

REAL NAME: Death **POWERS:** Near omnipotence, including the power to end the life of any being **FIRST APPEARANCE:** *Human Torch Comics* #5 (Sep 1941)

Death has existed for as long as the universe. It is a cosmic being that can take any form it chooses, often appearing in a skeletal human form or sometimes as a female humanoid. It is an abstract being in that it is a personification of one of the immutable laws of nature. Death has the power to end the life of any being but also the power to resurrect them. Above the Death of Earth-616 is Death of Death—a Multiversal being that passes judgment on the Deaths in each reality.

CHAOS AND ORDER

36   St
Cx
Chaos and Order

REAL NAME: Lord Chaos and Master Order **POWERS:** Near omnipotence, especially when combined **FIRST APPEARANCE:** *Marvel Two-in-One Annual* #2 (Dec 1977)

As their names suggest, Lord Chaos and Master Order personify the concepts of chaos and order. Although opposites, Chaos and Order are "brothers," and neither can exist without the other. Depending on the dominant state of the universe, either one can appear larger than the other. Although, in theory, they are less powerful than the Living Tribunal, they combine their powers to murder him when they feel he is failing to maintain the balance of the universe.

ANCILLARY EXEMPLARS

57   St
By
Beyonder

46   St
Ts
Stranger

53   St
Pf
Phoenix Force

58   St
Ob
Oblivion

60   St
Ey
Entropy

52   St
Eo
Eon

Sometimes apparently insignificant beings can have major effects on cosmic beings. The mysterious **Beyonder** becomes fascinated by the humans on Earth and studies them in order to discover more about his place in the Multiverse. The **Stranger**, creator of Ego the Living Planet, is also curious about Earth and its super-powered beings. The **Phoenix Force** is the embodiment of the universal life force and has frequently chosen a host from Earth. **Oblivion**, meanwhile, represents the state of nonexistence and has a close relationship with Death. **Entropy**, a child of the abstract being Eternity, personifies the Big Freeze—an aspect of the life cycle of the universe. Entropy later becomes Eternity. Another of Eternity's progeny is **Eon**, an abstract entity connected with the concept of time.

BLACK PANTHER

23	St
Bp	
Black Panther	

REAL NAME: T'Challa **POWERS:** Super-senses; knowledge-sharing with previous Black Panthers; King of the Dead; genius intellect **FIRST APPEARANCE:** *Fantastic Four* #52 (Jul 1966)

There are few heroes who embody as many different properties as T'Challa, the Black Panther. His formidable powers come from an array of sources, so he is not overreliant on any one factor. And when all the facets of his skill set are working together at full capacity, T'Challa is undoubtedly one of Earth's greatest heroes.

T'Challa is not just a hero but also a monarch. In his kingdom of Wakanda, rulers do not automatically inherit the throne or the Black Panther identity that goes along with it. They must prove themselves worthy. After passing a series of tests, only then are they anointed with the Heart-Shaped Herb that grants them their enhanced abilities. It is originally thought that the herb, only found in Wakanda, is a gift from the panther goddess, Bast. Later this fable is found to have a scientific explanation—the herb is mutated by Vibranium from a long-ago meteorite strike. Made into a poultice and applied to a worthy recipient, it causes senses to be heightened and muscles and ligaments to grow stronger yet more flexible.

Vibranium, found only in Wakanda and the Savage Land of Antarctica, is a key part of the Black Panther's powers. Not only has the metallic ore created the effects of the Heart-Shaped Herb, but it is also used to give Black Panther superior equipment and weapons with which to defend his people. The Panther's suit is made of a Vibranium weave, which absorbs the impact of attacks with no harm to the wearer. It has claws made from Antarctic Vibranium—an anti-metal that can shred any other type of metal—stealth capabilities, and force-field generation, among many other powers. It also carries Vibranium energy daggers that can be willed into different shapes or strengths.

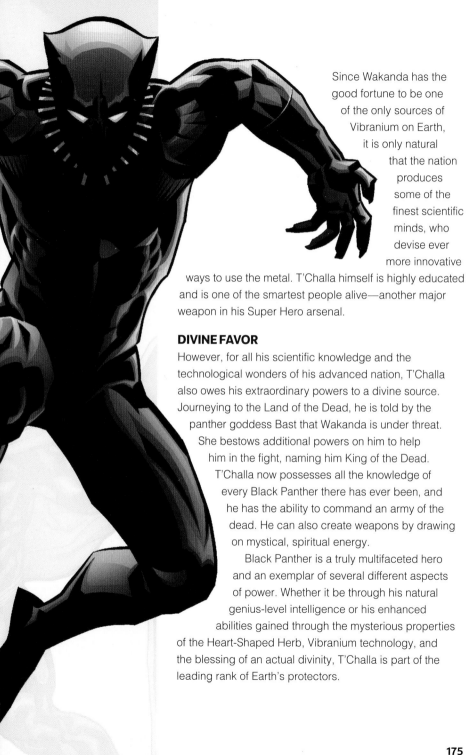

Since Wakanda has the good fortune to be one of the only sources of Vibranium on Earth, it is only natural that the nation produces some of the finest scientific minds, who devise ever more innovative ways to use the metal. T'Challa himself is highly educated and is one of the smartest people alive—another major weapon in his Super Hero arsenal.

DIVINE FAVOR

However, for all his scientific knowledge and the technological wonders of his advanced nation, T'Challa also owes his extraordinary powers to a divine source. Journeying to the Land of the Dead, he is told by the panther goddess Bast that Wakanda is under threat. She bestows additional powers on him to help him in the fight, naming him King of the Dead. T'Challa now possesses all the knowledge of every Black Panther there has ever been, and he has the ability to command an army of the dead. He can also create weapons by drawing on mystical, spiritual energy.

Black Panther is a truly multifaceted hero and an exemplar of several different aspects of power. Whether it be through his natural genius-level intelligence or his enhanced abilities gained through the mysterious properties of the Heart-Shaped Herb, Vibranium technology, and the blessing of an actual divinity, T'Challa is part of the leading rank of Earth's protectors.

DOCTOR STRANGE

8   St

Dc

Doctor Strange

REAL NAME: Stephen Strange **POWERS:** Astral projection, spell-casting, interdimensional travel, and telekinesis; near immortality **FIRST APPEARANCE:** *Strange Tales* #110 (Jul 1963)

There is no better exemplar of the properties of mystical powers than Stephen Strange—Earth's Sorcerer Supreme. At first, Strange does not know he is destined for this role, and he forges a career as a brilliant (though vain and materialistic) surgeon. After his hands are irreparably damaged in a car wreck, Strange begins a desperate hunt for a cure so that he can rebuild his surgical career. His last throw of the dice brings him to the Himalayas, where he seeks an individual called the Ancient One. Strange has heard this person has amazing powers. The Ancient One has also heard of Strange. He has been waiting for him ever since Strange was born, but instead of restoring his hands to full working order, he offers to teach him the mystic arts.

Overcoming his skepticism, Strange spends years learning as much as he can about magic from his tutor, harnessing powers both within himself and from external sources. He gains much of his power from channeling the energies of beings from other dimensions, including from the mystic entities Cyttorak, Hoggoth, and Agamotto. Strange acquires many magical artifacts from which he can also channel mystic powers. Among these are the Cloak of Levitation, which enables him to fly; the Orb of Agamotto, which reveals to him anything happening on Earth and in other dimensions; and a powerful volume of spells called the Book of the Vishanti.

One of Doctor Strange's most potent artifacts is the Eye of Agamotto, which bestows on him magical abilities. Usually worn as an amulet around his neck, the Eye is,

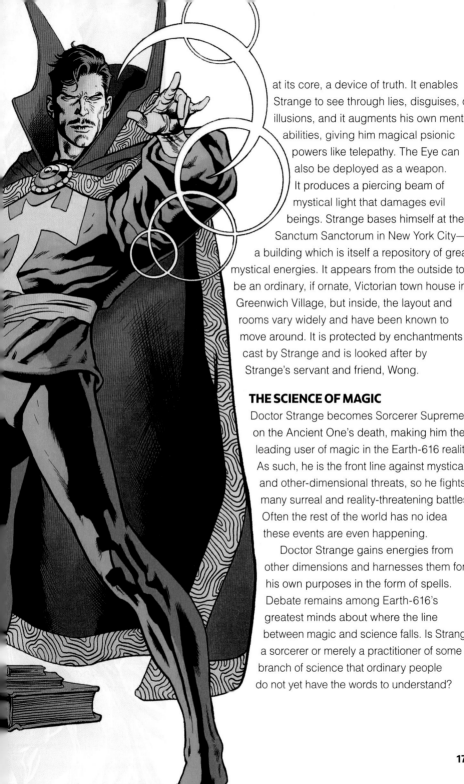

at its core, a device of truth. It enables Strange to see through lies, disguises, or illusions, and it augments his own mental abilities, giving him magical psionic powers like telepathy. The Eye can also be deployed as a weapon. It produces a piercing beam of mystical light that damages evil beings. Strange bases himself at the Sanctum Sanctorum in New York City— a building which is itself a repository of great mystical energies. It appears from the outside to be an ordinary, if ornate, Victorian town house in Greenwich Village, but inside, the layout and rooms vary widely and have been known to move around. It is protected by enchantments cast by Strange and is looked after by Strange's servant and friend, Wong.

THE SCIENCE OF MAGIC

Doctor Strange becomes Sorcerer Supreme on the Ancient One's death, making him the leading user of magic in the Earth-616 reality. As such, he is the front line against mystical and other-dimensional threats, so he fights many surreal and reality-threatening battles. Often the rest of the world has no idea these events are even happening.

Doctor Strange gains energies from other dimensions and harnesses them for his own purposes in the form of spells. Debate remains among Earth-616's greatest minds about where the line between magic and science falls. Is Strange a sorcerer or merely a practitioner of some branch of science that ordinary people do not yet have the words to understand?

SCARLET WITCH

REAL NAME: Wanda Maximoff **POWERS:** Magical powers include Chaos manipulation; reality-warping; psionic abilities; time manipulation **FIRST APPEARANCE:** *X-Men* #4 (Mar 1964)

12	St
Wh	
Scarlet Witch	

Wanda Maximoff is the Scarlet Witch and one of the best-known wielders of magic on Earth-616. She is an expert manipulator of a particular type of magic known as Chaos magic, although she is also very adept with other forms of the mystic arts. She has the ability to channel mystical energies and harness them as spells, which she calls her "hex" power.

Originally, it is thought that Maximoff's powers are from an X-gene, which would make her a mutant, but this is actually not the case. She and her speedster twin brother, Pietro, are experimented on by the obsessive geneticist the High Evolutionary. He then casts them aside with the cover story of being mutants to explain away their powers. Maximoff's ability to channel mystic energy was awakened and enhanced by the High Evolutionary, but not created by him.

REALITY SHOW

Maximoff and her brother Pietro, aka Quicksilver, come from a long line of sorcerers. To further enhance her powers, she is made a conduit of Chaos magic by the demon-god Chthon. She is regarded as one of the mightiest individuals on Earth, largely due to her ability to manipulate and change reality itself.

She can create an object or living thing from nothing, including her own mystical weapons. Conversely, she can also erase objects and living things from existence. Her illusions confuse and disorient opponents, and she has many, many more spells and psionic possibilities.

Scarlet Witch is an individual so powerful that she is thought to be the nexus point for the entire Earth-616 reality—a being through whom all mystical energies can flow and who can influence the future for everyone.

Wanda Maximoff's ability to channel mystical energy makes her powerful, but being able to warp reality is a responsibility that must be used carefully.

DOCTOR DOOM

REAL NAME: Victor von Doom **POWERS:** Magical powers include spell-casting; force-field creation; mind transference; genius intellect **FIRST APPEARANCE:** *Fantastic Four* #5 (Jul 1962)

3   Vo

Vd

Doctor Doom

Victor von Doom inhabits the nexus between science and magic. He inherits a propensity for magic from his mother, but he also possesses a genius-level intellect, particularly in the field of invention. While these are certainly part of the secret of his success, Doom's rise to power—he is the monarch of Latveria—can also be attributed to his extraordinary willpower and boundless ambition. Whereas his occasional failures could be laid at the door of his colossal arrogance.

Horribly scarred when one of his inventions goes wrong, Doom has an armored battle suit made that includes a face mask. Typically, this armor features both magical and technological elements and gives Doom extensive defensive and offensive capabilities. Doom also masters advanced forms of travel, including time travel and teleportation, and builds many Doombots. These are robots that can either do his bidding or take his place in certain situations. He can even transfer his mind to another body—an ability that has enabled him to escape death.

MAGIC TIME

Doctor Doom's ability to travel through time has enabled him to meet and learn from infamous magic-wielder Morgan le Fay. He channels most of his magical powers from the demonic Hazareth Three and through them is able to use a range of spells. Among many abilities, Doom can manipulate the elements, harness energy, create force-fields, and travel between dimensions.

Doctor Doom is a unique individual with some very special gifts, and it is not unknown for him to use them to help the people of Earth. However, the person Doom always helps first is himself, and generally he perceives others as many sheep to be ruled over.

Doctor Doom has magic, ambition, and a brilliant mind, but he is often hampered by his obsession with his nemesis, Reed Richards (Mister Fantastic).

DOCTOR VOODOO

REAL NAME: Jericho Drumm **POWERS:** Voodoo powers include spirit possession; fire resistance; manipulation; hypnosis **FIRST APPEARANCE:** *Strange Tales* #169 (Sep 1973)

30	St

Vo
Doctor Voodoo

A native of the country Haiti, Jericho Drumm is a practitioner of voodoo magic. When his brother is killed by an evil spell, Drumm leaves behind his career as a doctor and trains to be a Houngan—a voodoo priest. His teacher, Papa Jambo,

helps train him, but he also casts a spell that binds the spirit of Drumm's brother, Daniel, to him. This spirit can be used to make Drumm himself twice as strong or be sent out to possess others and bind them to Drumm's will. Drumm's voodoo abilities include being able to manipulate and be resistant to fire, conjure up magical smoke, teleport, and hypnotize others, primarily animals and plants. His powers come from the spirit gods of voodoo, known as the Loa, who are actually a race of beings from a pocket dimension called Orun.

CAPTAIN BRITAIN

REAL NAME: Brian Braddock **POWERS:** Super-strength, stamina, durability, agility, reflexes, and senses; flight; genius intellect **FIRST APPEARANCE:** *Captain Britain* #1 (Oct 1976)

35	St

B
Captain Britain

Brian Braddock becomes Captain Britain, the champion of his nation, when he is given the Amulet of Right by Merlin the sorcerer. Merlin is the son of a demon and Roma, a wizard's daughter. Braddock has the choice of the Amulet or the Sword of

Might, and he chooses the Amulet because he sees himself more as a thinker than a fighter. As Captain Britain, Braddock is endowed with super-powers that work by channeling energies from another dimension, including flight and super-strength. For a while, the Amulet is the conduit for his powers, but later it is Captain Britain's suit that channels the mystical energies. Some time later, Braddock has absorbed enough of the mystic energy himself to summon his powers on his own, although he must have belief in himself to do this.

THE ANCIENT ONE

9   St

On

The Ancient One

REAL NAME: Yao **POWERS:** Magical powers siphon energy from himself, the world, and other dimensions **FIRST APPEARANCE:** *Strange Tales* #110 (Jul 1963)

The Ancient One is born in the mystic Himalayan city of Kamar-Taj in the 15th century. As he grows, he learns about magic and discovers how to eradicate disease, poverty, and even death. He dedicates his long life to combating those who use magic for their own evil ends. Adept at feats such as astral projection, interdimensional travel, and telepathy, he is named the Sorcerer Supreme of Earth-616 by the cosmic being Eternity because he has greater magical knowledge than anyone else in his dimension.

WICCAN

41   St

Wc

Wiccan

REAL NAME: Billy Kaplan **POWERS:** Reality-warping, lightning manipulation, teleportation, flight, and telekinesis **FIRST APPEARANCE:** *Young Avengers* #1 (Apr 2005)

Wiccan's origins are a mystery and, so too, is the source of his magical power. He and his twin brother, Tommy Shepherd (Speed), are apparently reincarnations of the children wished into existence by the Scarlet Witch and part of the essence of the demon Mephisto. Wiccan has either inherited these powers or gained them some other way, as he too can warp reality and has demonstrated a wide range of other magical abilities. Wiccan is destined to become the omnipotent Demiurge and rewrite the rules of magic.

ANCILLARY EXEMPLARS

49   St

Ag

Agatha
Harkness

43   St

Du

Doctor Druid

54   St

Bl

Black Cat

50   Vo

Tg

Tigra

64   St

Ac

America Chavez

47   Co

Dy

Destroyer

Magic on Earth has a rich and storied history. **Agatha Harkness** is an ancient sorceress who is part of the Salem Witch Trials and later trains the Scarlet Witch. **Doctor Druid** is empowered by the Druidic tradition of Britain. Others look to the animal kingdom. **Black Cat's** jinx power comes from the Kingpin but is replaced by feline abilities. Catlike **Tigra** draws her powers from a magical amulet. **America Chavez** is from a dimension outside time and space, where she absorbs mystic energy from the cosmic being known as the Demiurge. On Asgard, the robotlike **Destroyer** is an enchanted suit of armor created by Odin.

DORMAMMU

REAL NAME: Dormammu **POWERS:** Vast range of abilities making him one of the most powerful mystical beings in existence; immortality **FIRST APPEARANCE:** *Strange Tales* #126 (Nov 1964)

17	Co
Du	
Dormammu	

Dormammu is an extradimensional demon of great power. He is originally a Faltine—a being comprised of pure mystical energy. He and his sister Umar search for solid matter to make themselves more powerful and to become the dominant beings in their dimension, but the gathering of solid material is forbidden and so they are cast out. Continuing his quest for greater power, Dormammu arrives in the Dark Dimension, from where he learns how to break into other dimensions and absorb them into his own. He also discovers that the Dark Dimension is full of potent mystical energies that he can use to enhance himself. After saving the Dark Dimension from the destructive Mindless Ones, Dormammu is appointed its ruler along with his sister, but he later traps her in another dimension to assume sole power.

DEMONIC ENERGY

Dormammu usually appears with a flaming head, which is a legacy of his Faltine origins. His nature as an energy

being means that it is extremely difficult to injure Dormammu in any way. He can manipulate the energy of his body into any shape or size. Because of his time spent in the Faltine and the Dark Dimensions, he has amassed vast magical abilities, which are particularly strong in his home realms. He can banish or summon individuals interdimensionally, harness energy to create living weapons, and even resurrect the dead, while he seems himself to be immortal. He takes a special interest in Earth-616 and has clashed with its protective Sorcerer Supremes many times. Despite his great powers, Dormammu does not always emerge victorious from these encounters.

Dormammu does not take kindly to finding Earthlings in his Dark Dimension, but he is always quick to use them as a way to achieve his conquering ambitions.

BARON MORDO

REAL NAME: Karl Mordo **POWERS:** Extensive magical powers include: energy manipulation; teleportation; levitation; astral projection **FIRST APPEARANCE:** *Strange Tales* #111 (Aug 1963)

11	Vo
Bn	
Baron Mordo	

Baron Karl Mordo is born into a Central European family who are actively seeking to practice black magic to reassert their powers in their homeland and return to the old ways. He trains with the Ancient One in the Himalayas but falls under the thrall of the dread Dormammu, sacrificing his family to win favor with the demon. Mordo is adept at channeling energy from within himself, from the wider universe, and from other dimensions in order to use it for magic. He can fire out energy blasts, separate from his own body using astral projection, teleport, levitate, and create force fields. Despite devoting his life to black magic, when Mordo discovers he has cancer, he repents and seeks forgiveness from those he has wronged. He dies but later reappears due to an interference in the timelines.

NIGHTMARE

REAL NAME: Nightmare **POWERS:** Conjures up illusions and reshapes his Nightmare Realm to stimulate fear, which he then feeds off **FIRST APPEARANCE:** *Strange Tales* #110 (Jul 1963)

10	Vo
Ng	
Nightmare	

Nightmare is a god-demon and the personification of nightmares. He originally hails from the higher dimension of Everinnye, but then he becomes the ruler of the Nightmare Realm in the Dream Dimension. He has great powers over sleeping beings. He abducts their astral forms and brings them to his realm, where he tortures them. He feeds on the psychic energies from these encounters. While he has hold of someone, he can discover their worst fears, meaning that Nightmare is one of the arcane group known as the Fear Lords. However, he has no power over those individuals who do not dream or those who have conquered their fears. When Nightmare becomes bored of his life, he takes a mortal form and opens a club on Earth to gain a new angle on the fears of humanity.

GHOST RIDER

REAL NAME: Johnny Blaze **POWERS:** Super-strength; hellfire manipulation; sin absorption; soul harvesting; Penance Stare; healing factor **FIRST APPEARANCE:** *Marvel Spotlight* #5 (Aug 1972)

27   Co

Gr

Ghost Rider

Motorcycle stunt rider Johnny Blaze makes a deal with the demon Mephisto in order to save the life of his terminally ill foster father. But when the man dies of another cause, Mephisto comes to collect anyway. Blaze is bound to the demon Zarathos, the spirit of Vengeance, who possesses him every night and transforms him into the Ghost Rider. In this form, Blaze's head appears to be a flaming skull, and he travels around on a fiery "Hell Cycle" looking for sinful souls to punish. Blaze has enhanced strength and endurance, and he can also fire blasts of a mystical flame he calls hellfire. Although Ghost Rider has demonic origins, he tries to be a force for good. Blaze is not the only Ghost Rider— there have been many. The latest is Robbie Reyes, who drives a Hell Charger car and has even become an Avenger.

BLACK KNIGHT

REAL NAME: Dane Whitman **POWERS:** Expert swordsman, usually wields the cursed Ebony Blade; skilled in science and engineering **FIRST APPEARANCE:** *Avengers* #47 (Dec 1967)

25   St

Dw

Black Knight

The Black Knight is the human Dane Whitman. He is not personally connected to a demon, but he wields a cursed sword. Known as the Ebony Blade, it is forged by the wizard Merlin from a substance called starstone as a counterpart to the pure Excalibur sword. Mystical properties enable it to cut through any substance, protect its wielder from death, and guard against magical attack. However, when it is used for evil acts, the malevolence of the deed is absorbed into the blade and transmitted to the wielder, fueling their bloodlust and leading to insanity. Whitman spends his life fighting against the Blade, choosing to take the responsibility himself rather than letting the weapon fall into the wrong hands. Yet he also enjoys the power it gives him, as without it he is just an ordinary human.

MEPHISTO

Mephisto

REAL NAME: Mephisto **POWERS:** Strength; healing factor; immortality; shape-shifting; reality manipulation **FIRST APPEARANCE:** *Silver Surfer* #3 (Dec 1968)

Mephisto is an enormously mighty demon whose history and behavior are closely intertwined with that of Satan in the Christian tradition. As is common with demonic beings, Mephisto is much more powerful within his own realm—known as Hell—than he is outside it. Although his powers are extensive, Mephisto has no power over others unless they allow him to. This means that his interactions with Earth's inhabitants frequently involve cutting deals with them, allowing him to get something of value from them while he apparently gives them something in return that they need or desire. Mephisto is an arch manipulator whose actions have reshaped Earth-616.

HELLSTROM

Hellstrom

REAL NAME: Daimon Hellstrom **POWERS:** Super-strength and soulfire via Darksoul; mystical abilities **FIRST APPEARANCE:** *Ghost Rider* #1 (Sep 1973)

Daimon Hellstrom is the child of the demon known as Satan and a human woman. His father hopes to use the child to enhance his power on Earth, but when Hellstrom grows up, he rejects Satan and devotes his life to battling his evil. Hellstrom inherits from his father a set of powers stemming from the "Darksoul"—a demonic counterpart to his human soul. Through this power, Hellstrom has super-strength and mystical abilities, including the ability to sense the presence of the supernatural and create and project "soulfire." However, he later loses his Darksoul. He has also been known to wield a trident made of a demonic metal that amplifies his soulfire powers.

ANCILLARY EXEMPLARS

Elektra

The Hood

Gargoyle

Deals with demons can happen by accident or by design. A demonic connection is part of the deal when **Elektra** is resurrected by the villainous clan of ninjas called the Hand. She is already a master assassin, but her link with the demonic force gives her heightened psionic powers, including the ability to seize control of the minds of others. Aspiring villain Parker

Robbins inadvertently gains demonic powers and becomes **The Hood** when he steals a cloak and boots that channel the energies of the dread demon Dormammu. The spirit of World War I veteran Isaac Christians is transferred to the body of a demon when he becomes **Gargoyle** in an effort to save his ailing hometown of Christiansboro, Virginia.

BLADE

REAL NAME: Eric Brooks **POWERS:** Super-strength, speed, stamina, durability, agility, and reflexes; longevity; healing factor **FIRST APPEARANCE:** *Tomb of Dracula* #10 (Jul 1973)

When his mother is fatally bitten by a vampire as she is giving birth to him, Eric Brooks's DNA is altered and he is born a Dhampir—half human, half vampire. This hybrid status gives Brooks all the perks of being a vampire—

including super-strength and longevity—with none of the drawbacks. He is a daywalker, undamaged by sunlight, and is immune to silver and crosses, which render true vampires weak. However, he does share a need to consume blood. He finds a way around this by nourishing his body with a serum that replicates blood. Brooks uses his advantages to become the vampire-hunter Blade, seeking vengeance for the death of his mother. While on this quest, he also battles other supernatural foes, at times teaming up with like-minded Super Heroes.

DRACULA

REAL NAME: Vlad Dracula **POWERS:** Super-strength, speed, stamina, durability, agility, and reflexes; immortality; shape-shifting **FIRST APPEARANCE:** *Suspense* #7 (Mar 1951)

Vlad Dracula is not the first vampire, but he becomes the most notorious. His name is synonymous with the bloodthirsty supernatural creatures. Born human in the 15th century in Transylvania, Dracula is forging a brutal career as a warlord when

he is badly wounded. Taken to a gypsy for healing, he is instead turned into a vampire. He now has the power to turn others into vampires using an enzyme found in his vampiric saliva. He also has a range of superhuman powers and is largely immortal, though he can be killed in a few specific ways. Dracula has the ability to shape-shift into creatures like bats or wolves, and he can also command lesser beings. Carrying his instinct to conquer into his vampire life, Dracula soon wins the title of Lord of Vampires by killing its previous incumbent.

THE HAND

FIRST APPEARANCE: *Daredevil* #174 (Sep 1981)

37	Vo
Hn	
The Hand	

The Hand is an ancient ninja clan that is originally linked with both Japanese nationalism and also with the worship of a demon known as the Beast. As the organization grows, it develops many factions, all of which seek power for themselves. The Hand also lends its acolytes out as assassins-for-hire. These members are practitioners of occult magic, capable of bringing the dead back to life and programming them to operate as a servant of the Hand. Anyone seeking to join voluntarily must pass a brutal initiation to prove they are willing to take and give out terrible pain in service to the Hand. As ninjas, they must be masters of stealth attacks and martial arts. The Hand is the longtime enemy of another clan of warriors called the Chaste.

JUGGERNAUT

REAL NAME: Cain Marko **POWERS:** Super-strength, stamina, and durability; unstoppable in motion; healing factor; immortality; force-field generation **FIRST APPEARANCE:** *X-Men* #12 (Jul 1965)

19	Vo
Ju	
Juggernaut	

While on a mission in Asia, bully Cain Marko is in the process of going AWOL from the army when he comes across a temple. Inside, he finds a gem belonging to the demon-god Cyttorak, which turns him into the super-strong Juggernaut, avatar of the demon. Marko's body becomes very durable, and he can create a force-field around himself for additional protection. Juggernaut is the archetypal "irresistible force," virtually unstoppable once in motion. After he loses the Gem of Cyttorak, Marko happens upon the Crimson Bands of Cyttorak. He bonds with them, regaining his abilities and also gaining a mystical suit of armor that he can summon at will. However, Marko no longer wants to do Cyttorak's bidding, and tries to forge a new path, regretful of the damage he has caused in the past.

IRON FIST

REAL NAME: Danny Rand **POWERS:** Super-strong punch; chi-enhanced stamina and reflexes; healing factor; master martial artist **FIRST APPEARANCE:** *Marvel Premiere* #15 (May 1974)

Chi is a life force that flows in every being in existence, but nobody can harness its power quite like Danny Rand, aka Iron Fist. After being orphaned, he spends a decade in the extradimensional city of K'un-Lun being trained in martial arts.

When he is deemed ready, Rand gains the power of the Iron Fist by defeating a giant mystical serpent and plunging his hands into its molten heart. As a result of this combat, the mark of the dragon is visible on his chest. He can now raise his chi to superhuman levels, focus it into his hands, and deliver a super-strong punch. His mastery of chi extends to all areas of his physicality so he can use it to enhance his durability, speed, and stamina, and even his senses. He also uses chi to heal himself and others or to establish an empathetic link.

STICK

REAL NAME: Unknown **POWERS:** Chi manipulation; heightened senses include a radar sense; master martial artist **FIRST APPEARANCE:** *Daredevil* #176 (Nov 1981)

Stick is an extremely mysterious individual. Even his real name is unknown. He simply goes by the name of his favorite weapon. He is blind but has worked on developing his other senses as a means of compensation. Stick is a master of chi manipulation, using it for a variety of purposes, including telepathic communication. He is a highly adept practitioner of martial arts. He trains the hero Daredevil in fighting techniques and in how to control and hone his senses after losing his sight. Stick leads the group of warriors called the Chaste whose mission is to oppose the evil Hand organization. He sacrifices himself to defeat the Hand in battle by absorbing his opponents' chi into himself. When the life energy overloads his body, he dies, but he is later resurrected by the Collector.

SHANG-CHI

32	St
Kf	
Shang-Chi	

REAL NAME: Shang-Chi **POWERS:** Peak-human strength and durability; master martial artist; chi manipulation **FIRST APPEARANCE:** *Special Marvel Edition* #15 (Dec 1973)

Shang-Chi is one of the world's greatest martial artists, having trained all his life to be the perfect assassin under the tutelage of his evil crime-lord father. But Shang-Chi has an innate sense of right and wrong, and so he leaves his father behind and goes out into the world to make his own way. As well as his martial-arts skills, Shang-Chi is also a master of harnessing chi, the spiritual energy that is present in all life-forms. He uses the chi within his own body to increase the strength of his strikes to extraordinary levels, enabling him to shatter rock-hard surfaces. Chi also renders him much more durable than regular humans and helps him heal more quickly from injuries.

COLLEEN WING

34	Vo
Cw	
Colleen Wing	

REAL NAME: Colleen Wing **POWERS:** Harnessing chi power; martial arts and swordsmanship skills **FIRST APPEARANCE:** *Marvel Premiere* #19 (Nov 1974)

Colleen Wing is a prime example of just how far a human can push themselves if they unlock their whole potential. Growing up in a mountainous region of Japan, Wing learns the ancient ways of the samurai from her grandfather. This means not only is she an expert in martial arts and swordsmanship, but she can also harness the powerful chi energy within her body to increase her strength and endurance levels as well as promote faster healing. After moving to New York City, Wing starts using her extensive skills as one of the Daughters of the Dragon—a private investigation team she founds with best friend and former NYPD police officer Misty Knight.

ANCILLARY EXEMPLARS

52	Vo
Dv	
Steel Serpent	

61	St
Td	
Tiger's Beautiful Daughter	

62	St
Po	
Prince of Orphans	

63	St
Pm	
Power Man	

The ability to harness chi transforms individuals into mighty warriors. Davos steals the power of Iron Fist, calling himself the **Steel Serpent**, and is later empowered as an Immortal Weapon—a representative of one of the seven capital cities of Heaven. Other Immortal Weapons include **Tiger's Beautiful Daughter**, who wields razor-sharp fans as well as chi powers, and **Prince of Orphans**, who can assume a gaseous form. Meanwhile, **Power Man** can absorb the chi energy of the world around him and use it to fight crime.

Senior Editor Cefn Ridout
Senior Designer Nathan Martin
Production Editor Siu Yin Chan
Senior Production Controller Mary Slater
Managing Editor Sarah Harland
Managing Art Editor Vicky Short
Publishing Director Mark Searle

Layout styling Lisa Lanzarini

Packaged for DK by Plum Jam
Editors Hannah Dolan and Elizabeth Dowsett
Designers Guy Harvey and Karan Chaudhary

First published in Great Britain in 2021 by
Dorling Kindersley Limited
One Embassy Gardens,
8 Viaduct Gardens, London SW11 7BW
A Penguin Random House Company

Dorling Kindersley Limited
DK, a Division of
Penguin Random House LLC
21 22 23 24 25 10 9 8 7 6 5 4 3 2 1
001–323476–Sep/2021

© 2021 MARVEL

The authorized representative in the EEA is
Dorling Kindersley Verlag GmbH. Arnulfstr. 124, 80636 Munich, Germany.

A CIP catalogue record for this book is available from the British Library.
ISBN 978-0-24150-083-5

Printed and bound in China

ACKNOWLEDGMENTS
DK would like to thank Julie Ferris; Melanie Scott for her text and expertise;
Brian Overton, Caitlin O'Connell, Jeff Youngquist, Lisa Montalbano, and Joe Hochstein
at Marvel for vital help and advice; and Jennette ElNaggar for proofreading.

For the curious

www.dk.com

This book is made from
Forest Stewardship Council™
certified paper—one small
step in DK's commitment
to a sustainable future.